Metrolink: The First 25 Years

Trams that reinvented the Original Modern City

Mark Ovenden

 Rails In association with:  Transport for Greater Manchester  Metrolink

Maps on pages 10, 15, 20, 38, 41, 47, 52, 63, 111 are Crown copyright reserved 2017, licence number 100059147.

ISBN 978-1-85414-415-7

Published by Rails Publishing in association with Transport for Greater Manchester
www.capitaltransport.com

Printed in the EU

Contents

Trams to all chapters

"In the time it takes to get from Bury to Victoria on Metrolink, the earth has travelled 45,000 miles around the sun"

Brian Cox, Astronomer

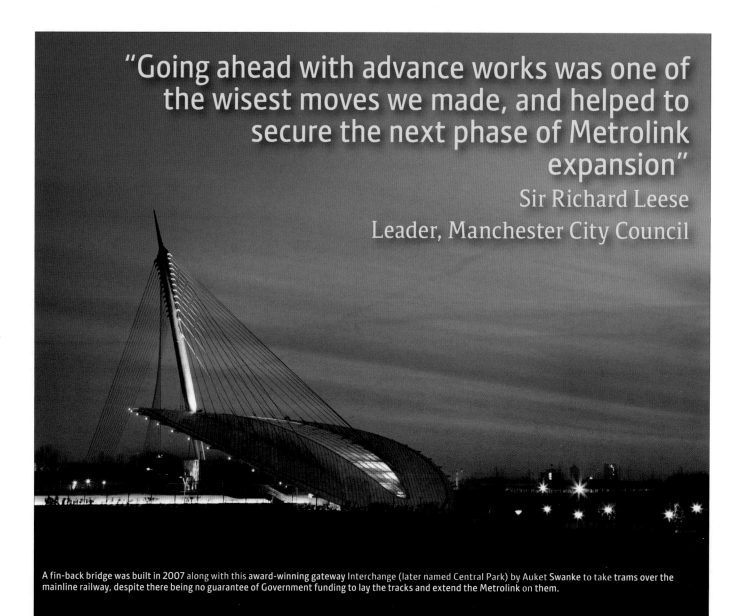

"Going ahead with advance works was one of the wisest moves we made, and helped to secure the next phase of Metrolink expansion"

Sir Richard Leese
Leader, Manchester City Council

A fin-back bridge was built in 2007 along with this award-winning gateway Interchange (later named Central Park) by Auket Swanke to take trams over the mainline railway, despite there being no guarantee of Government funding to lay the tracks and extend the Metrolink on them.

Foreword

Sir Richard Leese

The 2017 opening of the second city crossing highlights how much Manchester has changed in such a short space of time, and represents a major milestone in development and growth.

Sometimes we undervalue what we have achieved since government first cancelled our Big Bang expansion programme. The north always has to fight ferociously for every penny of central government money. Even getting the first route (Bury-Altrincham in 1992) was a battle. But we needed new lines to make Metrolink into a network and broaden the service to more of the conurbation.

That's why I was in favour of the Big Bang, doing it all in one go, and when Transport Secretary Alistair Darling announced that it was being scrapped, we adjourned a Council meeting, started an impromptu demonstration on St Peters Square stop and I demanded his resignation calling for him to "Move over Darling".

We recognised that costs had gone up, but Whitehall had taken so long dithering over approving the money it was no surprise. So we immediately launched the "Get Metrolink Back on Track campaign" and with the help of Tony Lloyd, Peter Smith (Leader of Wigan) and myself we re-established relationships with Darling. We maintained regular face-to-face behind the scenes dialogue with every subsequent Secretary of State for Transport – and there were a lot of them. I was fortunate to have a very good working relationship with the last of these, Andrew Adonis (I worked with him on high speed rail to Manchester and other issues). Good relationships help get through unnecessary bureaucratic blockages but you need a lot more than that to deliver schemes of this magnitude. You need robust business plans that demonstrate the transport case and the value for money case. Evidence!

To start with we were offered an alternative route for funding through the T.I.F. but it required unanimity of all 10 GM councils for it to be passed, and after the referendum we were forced into was lost – which cost a lot of time and money – we got the help of KPMG

Richard Leese at Urban Living Day, 2013.

and others to find a new form of economic analysis and the Greater Manchester Transport Fund was established to help leverage the money.

Now the completed Metrolink network is influential on development of the whole city region: it's allowed more people from all over the conurbation to get in to the city centre where jobs are. So more high value added employers come here: digital science and media to name a few. And you can get to any point on the network with just one change. We're now looking at our heavy rail and the bus network problems caused by deregulation: Falling off the cliff was easy, climbing back up takes longer. And in another 25 years: we should see tram-trains, possibly some kind of orbital route, a third city centre crossing (will have to be underground). Transport itself will change. Driverless cars, transport on demand. Fewer people will need to own their own vehicles. Expect expansion.

If we're convinced; we find a way. The Manchester Way.

How the city was traversed by trams in the early 1900s. The central building is the old hospital – now the site of Piccadilly Gardens tram stop and bus station.

The First Generation

Trams to South-East Lancashire & North-East Cheshire

Due in part to the rapid industrialization of what was effectively the world's first modern city, Manchester and the surrounding towns were early adopters of many innovative technologies. The method of transporting the burgeoning throngs around an ever expanding urban space was one of them: and in many senses also a driver of the growth itself. While its claim to the first inter-city passenger train service (the Liverpool & Manchester Railway of 1830) is well established, its lead in omnibuses and trams is less appreciated.

Tollgate keeper John Greenwood (1788-1851) is now acknowledged as beginning Britain's first horse-omnibus service in 1824 (predating more documented operations in Paris and London). Running between Pendleton at the edge of Salford to Market Street in Manchester, his vehicles were so effective that Greenwood hired several omnibuses and developed other routes. The idea was also copied by other providers: 64 omnibuses were running from outlying towns into the centre of Manchester by 1850. Greenwood's operation allied itself with several of the other principal services in 1865 to create the Manchester Carriage Company. In 1877 they won the right to operate a brand new service. Not by this time more buses: but along the steel rails of the Manchester & Salford Tramway which had just been laid into the roads. Fast forward to the dawn of the new century and this company was operating 515 tramcars (needing the services of more than 5000 horses) over 140 route miles.

Going electric

Between 1901 and 1949 Manchester Corporation Tramways (MCT) was the operator of electric tram services. By 1928 it carried 328 million passengers on 953 trams, along 46 routes on 292 track miles.

The services operating in and around Manchester provided the United Kingdom's second largest tram network (those of 16 opera-

Horse drawn trams, here in the 1890s, popularised rails in the streets.

tors across the capital were combined in 1933 by the London Passenger Transport Board). Other large systems were in Glasgow (which had 100 miles of double track at its peak) and Birmingham (80 miles). The central and south central Manchester area probably had the densest concentration of tram services of any urban area in Britain. MCT services ran up to the edge of routes provided by other operators in (what is now) termed Greater Manchester, and in some instances had running rights over their lines and vice versa. There were extensive neighbouring systems in Salford, Oldham, Ashton & Hyde, Middleton, Rochdale, Bury, Bolton, Wigan and elsewhere.

Services were withdrawn earlier than most other British cities to be replaced by trolleybus and motor buses. Trams did not return to the city until the modern light-rail system Manchester Metrolink opened in 1992. The full history of this period is amply covered by other works (Bibliography, p. 127) but more relevant to the history

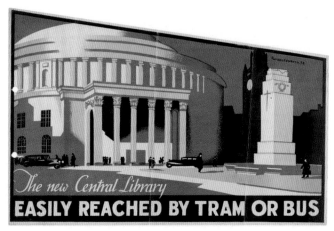

Posters like these advertising Manchester Corporation tram services were often displayed in buses too during the 1920s and 30s.

of the Metrolink itself is the city's fascinating history of proposed mass rapid transit services which are very much part of the roots of the Metrolink story.

The first underground almost happened here

There have been not just one, but around two dozen proposals to build a rapid transit system in Manchester including the 1839 tunnel which would have been the world's first, but the only one which ever got started was the infamous Picc-Vic. The city became virtually encircled by railway stations and tracks laid on brick arches following the arrival of the world's first passenger service (between here and Liverpool) in 1830. By the 1900s there were four major terminals (Central, Exchange, London Road and Victoria) and as many goods stations, but none of them penetrated right into the heart of the city (a problem also shared by London, New York, Paris and other older cities where rail services were introduced after the central area had been built up). The biggest incentive for making improvements to railway connections in Manchester was always to try and link up the disparate termini stations. Some concepts focused on taking full size mainline trains from Victoria beneath the city centre to Piccadilly, others by making tunnels to run the surface level trams in between the main rail stations, and yet further plans were for a full scale underground railway network like London's or a circle line like the Glasgow Subway (which opened in 1896). Several of these proposals received

parliamentary approval and one got tantalizingly close to being built, and its ramifications play a crucial role in Metrolink's' story.

Two dozen dead ends

1839-42: First tunnel under the city centre proposed by the Liverpool & Manchester Railway to make a link from their planned Hunts Bank station (renamed Victoria when opened in 1844) to Manchester and Birmingham Railway's forthcoming Store Street station (opened in 1842, which was renamed London Road in 1847, and later Piccadilly). There are no details of any intermediate stations but it remained a dream.

1868: The City Railways company submission to Parliament: the Underground City Railway would run between Mount Street via Albert Square to Fallowfield and Withington Park. [1.]

1878: Manchester City Railway. A short section of tracks in a pair of brick lined tunnels (constructed using a tunnelling shield) about 24 foot below the surface was proposed between Blackfriars Street (for Exchange station) and the junction of Lees Street and Piccadilly (for London Road station). There would be one intermediate station at the junction of High Street and Market Street. The proposers of the Bill believed that the new line would "confer a great deal of benefit upon the town generally by relieving the present overcrowded street traffic and providing a rapid, frequent and cheap means of communication between the important railway stations". Although steam propulsion would have been the only option at this time, the idea was not opposed by the council when it assessed the Bill in December 1878. However no further mention is made of this idea. [2]

1901: Manchester City Circle Railway, a proposal for a 14 station circuit to be known of as a 'Tube Railway' The company was incorporated but the concept was costed at £1.5 million and did not move beyond the drawing board.

1903: Manchester Underground Railway, an ambitious tram tunnel scheme approximately 2 miles long with 9 portals by the mainline stations at Central, London Road, Victoria, and Oxford Road, plus others at Blackfriars Bridge & Victoria Bridge, Ancoats approach & Oldham Rd, and London Road approach. The major interchange station would be below the Royal Infirmary (now site of Piccadilly Gardens). It was costed in 1903 at "less than" £750,000.

1903: Revised underground scheme for trams on three lines. Architect and Engineer Mr. W.A. Jackson submitted his proposal to the Parliamentary sub-committee of Manchester City Council suggesting the cost would be £750,000 if single deck cars are used [3]. The price for construction big enough for double deck cars was not given. The idea was not progressed.

Circle Tube Railway plan from 1901. (Right) July 1903 tram tunnel plan.

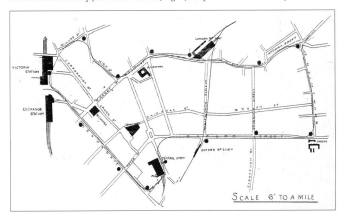

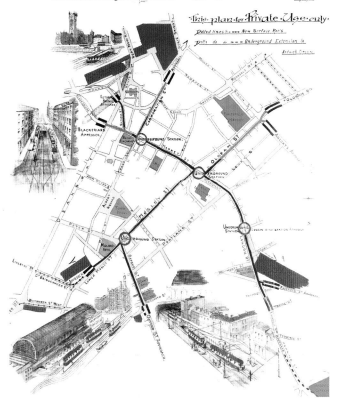

1911-12: Revised circle line with future branch to serve the University. Would have run: Victoria station, High St, Market St, Piccadilly, London Road station, Altrincham St, Charles St, Oxford Road station, (triangular junction laid for future branch to Whitworth Park), Central station, Deansgate, Victoria.

1912: Bowes subway. The City Tramways committee appointed a new sub-committee under Alderman Bowes to report on street widening, a new marshalling yard and the construction of subways for tramway traffic. Bowes Committee reports later that year they are "going forward with the proposal for the construction of underground systems". [4]

1914: Mr. J. McElroy, General Manager of Manchester Tramways reports to the Bowes committee that an underground solution will be too costly, but the Manchester Guardian published a sketch of what a scheme could look like anyway. [5]

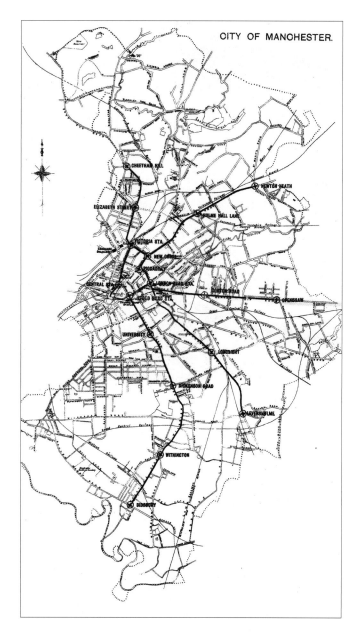

CITY OF MANCHESTER.

1924: Draining of the Irwell loops. An ambitious plan to redirect the river (which separates Manchester from Salford) in the city centre. It envisaged that the dry course could be used as a new road and underground tram route.

1925-26: Manchester City Council Underground Railways Special Committee studies a £4 million scheme to link the city centre with the suburbs including Salford and Prestwich.

1927-30: Underground Railway Special Committee final report. Chairman James Bowie's most ambitious proposal evolved from various ideas pushed in the 1920s. Summarised in the City Engineers report of October 1927 the map it shows five suburban lines feeding in to an inner circle of seven centrally located stations. The report explains that Line 1 to Didsbury could eventually be extended to Northenden and Wythenshawe. Line 2 to Levenshulme could be taken out to Stockport. Line 3 to Openshaw could later serve Droylsden and Audenshaw. Line 4 would not always terminate at Newton Heath: it could run to Failsworth and Oldham. And Line 5's short run to Cheetham Hill would offer the chance to take it to Prestwich. Almost the entirety of the 35 mile route was proposed to run in tunnel, serving 21 new stations at a cost then of almost £11 million.

1928: Mattinson's alternative scheme. Having considered the cost to be prohibitive, a more modest 7 miles from Tramways Manager Henry Mattinson suggested just two tunnels in the central area with no inner circle and no new suburban routes. One tunnel would run from near Trafford Bar through Cornbrook, serving Central station and Albert Square (where there would be an interchange) and on to Victoria emerging at Collyhurst. The other tunnel would run from near to present day Salford Crescent via an interchange at Albert Square through Piccadilly to London Road station, emerging after Chancery Lane in Ardwick. This plan collapsed as it required electrification of all connecting lines which rival companies would not pay for.

(Opposite): 1927 proposal. (Above): Evocative mid 1930s view of trams dominating Piccadilly.

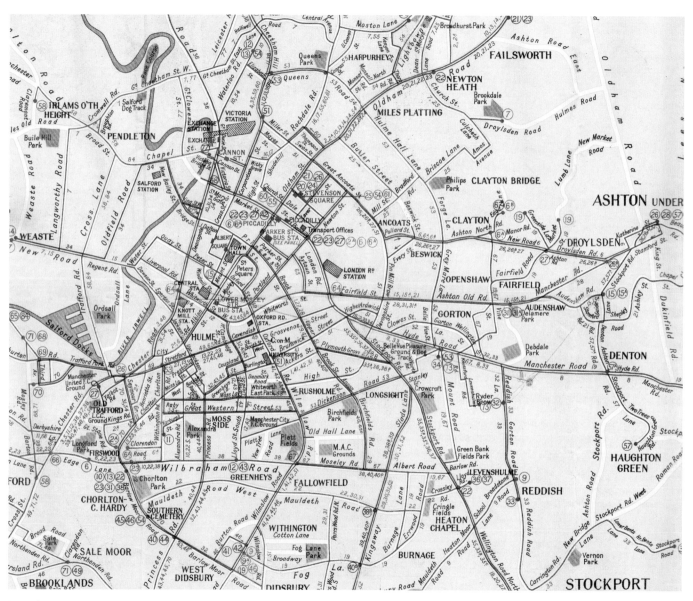

Detail from early 1940s Manchester Corporation Transport map. Although some had been converted to bus or trolleybus, remaining trams are shown in blue.

1967 Duorail proposal by WEI/Metro-Cammell.

1934: Alderman Bowie's revised plan. Not progressed.
1936: New overground station to be known as Gaythorn and new underground ones at Mayfield, Piccadilly, Exchange and New Cross. 8 miles. This scheme was not progressed.
1937: Manchester Corporation suggested nucleus of system at cost of between £6-7million. [6.]
1939: City Council review of tramway operations and proposal to abandon all in favour of trolleybuses and motor buses.
1945: Post-war plan. Trinity station – merger of Salford Central, Exchange and Victoria. Not progressed.
1949: The last Manchester corporation tram ran and faith in trolleybuses and buses seemed to derail tunnel plans.
1955: British Rail plan to rationalise services.
1962-63: SELNEC, Highway Plan reports that rail and/or rapid transport needed further work so establishes SELNEC Area Land-use Transportation Study (SALTS).
1963: Traffic In Towns report proposes elevated pedestrian walkways (one was built between Blackfriars Street and Victoria Bridge Street – demolished in 1996).
1964: Closure plan for Exchange station causes underground links to be revisited [7.]
1965: Light Railway Transport League (became LRTA)/ Manchester Area Rapid Transit Investigation Committee (MARTIC) scheme proposes a 'DuoRail' system of elevated, tunnelled and surface route between Bury and Ringway Airport with 8 station underground city centre circle

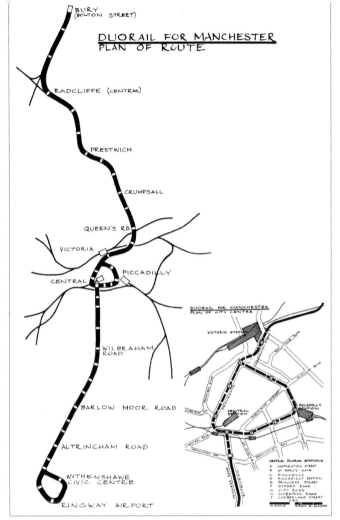
Although dating from 1965 these MARTIC proposals are interesting in comparison to what was eventually built as Metrolink.

1965: SELNEC Transportation Study began. Heywood and Royton MP Joel Barnett then Chief Secretary to the Treasury, and leader of the Picc-Vic pressure group, admitted costs would be enormous [8.]
1966-68: SALTS establishes Manchester Rapid Transit Study (MRTS) to look at feasibility of 11 mile line mostly underground, from Northenden to Higher Blackley (and East Didsbury branch). Although costs estimated at £50 million it receives Whitehall backing. [9.]

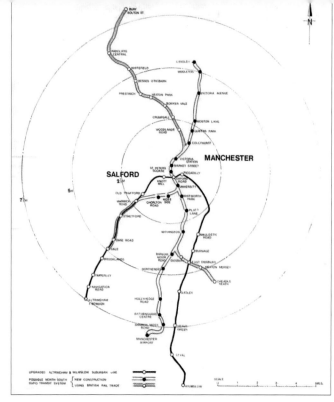

SELNEC's 1967 rapid transit plan, later modified into Picc-Vic.

Cover of GMC's 1970s brochure for Picc-Vic.

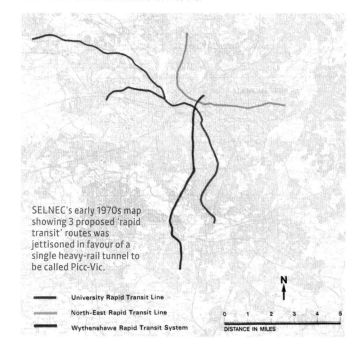

SELNEC's early 1970s map showing 3 proposed 'rapid transit' routes was jettisoned in favour of a single heavy-rail tunnel to be called Picc-Vic.

———— University Rapid Transit Line

———— North-East Rapid Transit Line

———— Wythenshawe Rapid Transit System

N

0 1 2 3 4 5
DISTANCE IN MILES

1969: SELNEC Rail Planning Study changed the emphasis from rapid transit to a heavy rail tunnel with a central section linking existing but electrified suburban services would offer better value for money. This was the kernel of the Picc-Vic scheme.

1972: Parliamentary approval gives SELNEC the power to plan and build the tunnel for a target opening date of 1978. [10.]

1973: Project named Picc-Vic to form centre of a sixty mile network, with 2.75 mile of twin bored tunnel and 5 stations underground. Initial forecast £21.5m is revised to £40m by year end [11]

1974: Government shelved the decision on the start date as costs predicted to be £105m. [12.]

1975: Last nail in coffin for Picc-Vic: grants approved to GMC were far below the amount needed. [13.]

1977: Picc-Vic formally abandoned.

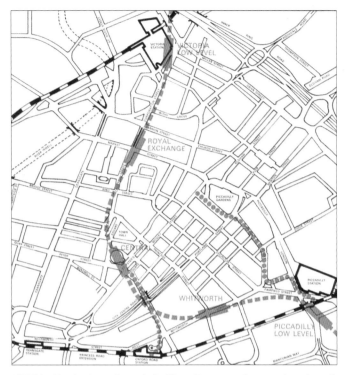

1973 Picc-Vic plan (tunnels are dashed lines 'Passenger Conveyors' are dotted).

How the Picc-Vic tunnel almost saw light

As can be seen from the exhaustive list, copious ideas had surfaced by which to join the city's disparate stations but following on from the various reports noted above, by the start of the 1970s all plans had been crystallised by the then Public Transport Executive (PTE) called 'SELNEC'. This clumsy amalgamation was formed by the areas that covered the Manchester conurbation (South East Lancashire and North East Cheshire), most of which was later integrated into a proper metropolitan county. The SELNEC PTE were required by a 1968 statute (like their equivalents in the other major cities) to come up with an infrastructure plan for future; and what was their solution? To construct a subterranean link between the two remaining major mainline British Rail termini (Victoria, to the north of the central area and Piccadilly to the south east) via a new £21.5 million twin bore tunnel under the city centre with three

Screaming 1970s minimalism, Fricker's sketches for Picc-Vic platform and concourse by architects EGS gave some idea of the design philosophy.

intermediate stations at Whitworth Street (for Oxford Road rail station), St Peter's Square (to be named Central) and Royal Exchange A strangely familiar trajectory to Mancunians considering the previous century's proposals.

Local Government re-organisation was on the horizon and following the perceived success of the capital-wide authority (Greater London Council, GLC, and its 33 metropolitan boroughs – created in 1965), the 1972 Act made provision for England's five remaining biggest conurbations to form metropolitan counties which among other things would assume powers for local transport. Most of SELNEC was absorbed into what became the 10 boroughs of Greater Manchester Council (GMC), which decided to continue pressing ahead with the Piccadilly-Victoria scheme.

Advanced studies began in 1971 with test bores and even aerial surveys starting in April 1972. The full cost of the tunnels alone was estimated at almost £93 million in 1973 prices when the first major report was published The Manchester scheme roughly coincided with ambitious plans in the new Tyne & Wear PTE's proposals for their Metro system and the Merseyside PTE beginning work on a single deep-level tunnel linking central Liverpool railway stations to each other.

Sir Robert Thomas, Fred Mulley, George Mann and Angus Munro examine one of the perspex cutaways of the proposed Piccadilly lower level station.

Preliminary plans and passenger conveyors

After decades of failed and more grandiose schemes this modest proposal looked the most likely of all to succeed. Instead of a straight line between Piccadilly and Victoria the opportunity was taken to make an arc which would provide three intermediate underground stations. In order for the tunnels to get to St Peter's Square ('Central' station) they would effectively miss the retail core and the main bus station at Piccadilly Gardens, so a long underground 'passenger conveyor' (which would most likely have been a series of travelators) was proposed to bring people to Piccadilly station – and another equally long one would link St Peter's Square to Oxford Road station.

With hindsight these would have been quite bizarre constructions (and both longer than if they had been put into other, closer Picc-Vic stations) and presumably would have involved a disruptive, lengthy and messy cut'n'cover digging-up of many key road arteries. As Brook and Dodge point out[14], the travelator subways were never properly developed into full architectural drawings, so perhaps these could be seen as an attempt to mitigate the failure of numerous attempts to locate the stations centrally?

Optimism high

Extremely detailed plans were however produced for the railway operations, including what were undoubtedly very expensive surveys of both the land through which the tunnels would pass and the surface links and electrification work needed to bring the tracks below ground from both Piccadilly and Victoria (no mean feat). A substantial number of alterations were planned to the existing old suburban rail network including a complete remodelling of the Bury interchange which was one of the few schemes that were completed ahead of the tunnelling work. Some track work was also completed at Altrincham. The original architects proposed (RL Moorcroft) who had designed London's Euston station, were replaced by a Manchester firm called Essex Goodman Suggitt (ESG) and they drew up many detailed plans and artists impressions of the

Created as a promotional display unit, this back-lit sign of the proposed Picc-Vic route was once on public view at Piccadilly station.

'Central' underground station entrance, beside the Library.

proposed stations mostly painted by David Fricker. As it would have been without doubt the biggest civil engineering project to happen in Manchester for decades, the plans also made provision for some large scale redevelopment of run-down buildings into new offices – and several would have their own subways leading to stations (e.g.: the proposed Heron House on Brazennose Street).

The vast Arndale Centre was also under construction at this time and several voids were left deliberately to accommodate various passageways from the proposed platforms of Royal Exchange station beneath. These have become the stuff of urban myth and some photographs have emerged in recent years of empty spaces created in the 1970s which could have been used for passengers walking between the station and Arndale shops.

Bore holes and bulldozers

A number of dilapidated buildings were also pulled down to make way for the proposed entrances and land at the corner of Whitworth Street and Princess Street has still yet to receive a replacement building on the site of those that had been demolished for Picc-Vic. Photographs of the bore holes near to this station also survive as a number of subterranean obstacles existed close to here (not least of

which was a culverted brook and an old canal tunnel). Although the trains themselves were never ordered, various speculative sketches were made of what was proposed to be a new high density multiple unit. One drawing of the vehicle even bore a striking resemblance to a London Underground 1967 Stock train for the Victoria line, but it would more likely have resembled the BR 445/446 class (later named as the 316, though despite specifications having been made by BREL, they were never produced).

Another source of speculation was the logo to be used or even the name: despite it being called 'Picc-Vic' openly for some years, it was also once called the SELNEC Picc-Vic Line and Brook and Dodge have found some evidence that a second tunnelled route the Knott Mill Line was mooted on a few drawings, presumed to run from what is now Deansgate station to Altrincham, so how to name it all?

Government blinks, Manchester loses

On 8th August 1973, John Peyton, Minister for Transport Industries, delivered what transpired to be the first in a series of central government knocks to the scheme stating: "there is no room for a project as costly as Picc-Vic before 1975/76 at the earliest." [14.] But when Whitehall's new financing process was in place Picc-Vic was again rejected. Transport Minister Fred Mulley had supported the project but neglected to mention it in the next year's funding round. Despite major lobbying from Manchester and the creation of new perspex models of the stations, road-building had become the Department of the Environment's new focus.

By 1977 even the GMC realised the game was up. In terms of the sheer person-hours, surveys and reports produced, the cancellation of Picc-Vic is without doubt the biggest unrealised rapid transit scheme outside London (which had suffered its own abandoned construction when the Northern Heights project was not fulfilled just after the Second World War [15.]). But the Manchester loss had an unforeseen fortuitous side, as the next decade would reveal.

"If it hadn't been for my holiday snaps of Italy, I wonder if the Metrolink would have happened in quite the way it did"
David Tibke, Light rail specialist

T68 Light Rail Vehicle undergoes final testing beside the original Market Street stop, April 1992.

The Second Generation

Trams to return to UK streets

Many commentators believe that had it not been for the cancellation of the Picc-Vic scheme in the 1970s, the more modest plan which later transpired for surface based light rail in Manchester would never have materialised and the resurrection of modern tramways in the UK could have been a lot slower.

All the issues that Picc-Vic aimed to tackle continued to be unresolved by its cancellation: Manchester was by far the largest British urban centre lacking cross-city rail links, and all the statutory obligations (instigated by the 1968 Transport Act to give Public Transport Executives grants to build major infrastructure) remained in place. Councillor Andrew Fender remembers the atmosphere at the time: "I'd watched with sadness the cancellation of Picc-Vic but we all understood that there would still need to be a radical re-think of rail transport for the regional centre". [16.] One Greater Manchester County Council (GMC) officer had been charged with looking what could be seen as. On a serendipitous holiday to Italy and Germany in 1981 David was struck by the effectiveness of the trams he saw, which sparked a radical idea for Manchester.

The Cinderella lines

GMC was becoming increasingly vexed by the subsidies it was paying to British Rail (BR) for the suburban lines (about 50p per rail passenger compared to 1p for bus) and with BR's focus on the planned Windsor link and Hazel Grove chord, it looked like passengers on the lines to Rochdale, Bury, Altrincham and Marple would endure years of worsening services for higher costs. Inside GMC they were even known of as the 'Cinderella lines': rolling stock was virtually life-expired, the electrical systems on the Bury and Altrincham lines were clapped out; all the other routes (with the exception of Glossop and Hadfield) remained un-electrified, and there was still no rail connection between Piccadilly and Victoria. After years in planning, BR did eventually build the short Windsor link by 1988, but it was never intended to bring rail services any

Class 504 slam-door rolling stock at Heaton Park on the BR Bury line.

closer to the heart of the city centre and it looked set to cause congestion on the cramped, long, brick viaduct between Deansgate and Piccadilly. As this busy double-track elevated section could not be quadrupled, the need would actually intensify to divert some local trains off it and allow them to cross the city centre in another manner. As a result planners inside BR had long-since come full circle to reconsider the possibility of tunnelling.

GMC formed policy to address the issue in November 1981. Inspired by his European visits, David Tibke wrote a paper entitled: Light rail for Greater Manchester as a complement to the Windsor link and gave it to his GMC colleagues including Tony Young in January 1982. It circulated to Greater Manchester Passenger Transport Executive (GMPTE) where planning director Angus Munro saw virtue in it.

Study Group has a bright idea

By February of 1982, in association with BR and GMPTE, the GMC formed a joint Rail Study Group (RSG) with the objective of developing a longer-term strategy to link the existing radial routes (the so-called Cinderella lines) through the central area of the city. The committee was chaired by Councillor Andrew Fender who recalled to the author that in a climate when rail expansion was completely

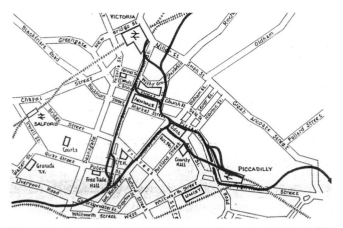
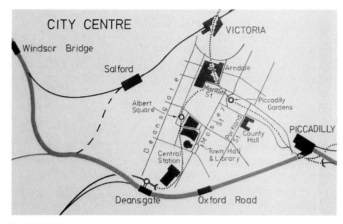

(Above): Routes considered in 1982 to traverse the centre by light rail. (Top Right): 1983 RSG report map showing a conventional tunnelled option.

off the national agenda "we had one shot at this: the worst case scenario was that rail transport faced being dismantled altogether, so there was an urgency to do something". [17.]

Routes examined

The RSG focused on the conversion of six BR suburban commuter lines (five physically separated from each other but still operational and one abandoned under the Beeching era of 1960s branch line closures). These would be connected to each other by means of new link built through or under central Manchester. The five BR lines would all need to be electrified to the same standard so the existing electrical equipment on the lines to Altrincham and Bury and that of the Glossop and Hadfield route would need to be replaced. The closed line would need to be re-laid with track and electrified from scratch. Six short disparate lines would then form three longer routes each penetrating directly into and crossing through the city:

• The Bury line would need to enter the central area from Victoria to get to Piccadilly where it would access Rose Hill and Marple lines.
• The Altrincham line would need to cross the city centre via Piccadilly to then head towards Glossop and Hadfield.
• The line from Rochdale via Oldham (often known as the 'loop line') would break free from its terminus in Victoria heading across the city centre area and accessing the (former, closed) railway line to Didsbury.

The location of the current termini of the five operational routes suggested that the most logical path to achieve any new link between them would be from southwards from Victoria and north-westwards from Piccadilly stations and north eastwards from a point between Trafford Bar and Deansgate stations: the three sections would thereby meet somewhere around Piccadilly Gardens/Market Street, more-or-less forming a slanted 'T'-shape in the city centre. Such a trajectory was also proposed several times on the previously envisaged schemes (See Chapter 1). Technical assistance was provided to the RSG by consultants Mott, Hay and Anderson (now: MottMcDonald) who had impressive credentials on London Underground projects, the Mersey rail tunnel and the Channel Tunnel. David Graham was at that time the GMPTE Director General and it was he who authorised that three working parties should be formed to examine the possible modes for achieving this. Councillor. Fender again: "There was still huge emotional attachment to the Picc-Vic scheme, but a realisation that some form of light-rail might also work". [18.]

Light rail not so new

While the concept of tunnelled metro systems was of course first established in the UK (London, 1863/1890 etc), 'Light Rail Transit' (in the modern context) was less well known. However the term 'light rail' was already in the ether as a viable option for mass rapid transit in Britain, both inside and outside the capital. The Tyne & Wear Metro system (opened in 1980 and classified as a light rail

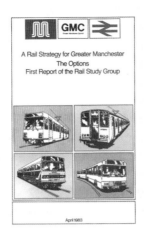

Front covers of the first and second Rail Study Group reports.

Revised image from the front cover of the 1984 RSG report.

operation, despite appearances), and Liverpool's Merseyrail loop/ link line (opened in 1977 and thought of as a heavy-rail suburban service with metro-like qualities) – both planned at the same time as Manchester's Picc-Vic – were proving rather successful. But a more radical, driverless, automated light metro service for London's regenerating old docklands was perhaps the boldest attempt to solve urban transport problems differently in Britain at that time.

The Docklands Light Railway (later rebranded as DLR) did not begin operation until 1987 but Manchester transport planners and the RSG had been keeping a keen eye on its progress. The mostly derelict and vast area of former docks east of the City were also the location of a cancelled heavy rail metro scheme: the curtailed Fleet Line. It eventually opened only as far as Charing Cross (as the Jubilee Line); so the London Docklands Development Corporation (LDDC) were investigating alternatives to bring people into the sites they wanted to regenerate. A 'people-mover' had been mooted in the 1970s, but during research in the early 1980s, the LDDC came down in favour of a light-rail scheme from close to Fenchurch Street mainline station to a point at the end of the Isle of Dogs. Initial construction contracts to begin work clearing old former rail track beds were awarded in 1984. The RSG were fully aware of these developments and their raising of the concept of light rail for Manchester would prove as radical its own way as the LDDC's scheme for London's Docklands.

The Railway Study Group reports

After six months of deliberating over the various tunnelled, busway and street track options, the RSG issued its first report in Spring 1983. Its three working parties had compared each potential mode in terms of reliability, hourly passenger flow, vehicle speed and acceleration, environmental impacts, the engineering costs of conversions and how each might be able to expand in the medium and long term future. GMC Chief Executive Tony Harrison oversaw it and Tony Young who chaired Working Party B looked at the bus angle, and concluded early on that most unguided bus (i.e. traditional buses) and trolleybus systems would not provide enough capacity given the expected demand. As with traditional street-running trams, the bus options were also perceived as not being able to reach the required speeds of around 80km/h amongst other road traffic. The impact in the landscape of monorail infrastructure ruled this option out as well – not to mention the cost – which was an additional issue also for the expensive rubber-tyred metro technology at the time. Some other automated vehicle guideway modes were also rejected. Three serious options were left:

• **Segregated busways** which could use articulated buses (or at least vehicles with enhanced passenger carrying capacity), and guided busways, but their disadvantage was that both would

Utrecht trams impressed RSG visitors with their high-floor steps.

require the old steel rails to be taken up on the five commuter lines (Didsbury route having closed to passengers in 1967).

• Tunnelled Metro, or Light Rail Transit (LRT) would involve electrifying all the suburban lines and building tunnels under the centre to join them together (effectively creating a heavy rail metro-type system – the so-called 'son of Picc-Vic'), or:

• Surface Light Rail: attempting the same connections as above but via on-street based tracks or guideways.

Two major and surprising issues arose about the cost of busways compared to train: firstly the capital expenditure of removing the rails and track bed (ballast) was more expensive than simply converting them for other rail use. Second, as a single light rail vehicle or a metro train could carry many more passengers than any bus, providing additional bus vehicles and the drivers for each one would be more expensive than the staffing costs of a smaller number of LRT or metro vehicles. In addition, consideration was given to bus passengers being forced to stand during peaks and the realisation that due to the nature of the station spacing and time for standing at high speed, a rail vehicle would be better for passenger comfort than a bus. The biggest impediment to a busway however was the nature of the guide rail or track itself: due to its need to be ether sunken lower than the road surface, or for the guide to protrude above the surface, it would require total segrega-

tion and there would be no way to make this practical in the centre of a busy city's streets. The conclusion was that a light rail system with a track that sits at the same level as the roadway and can be passed over by other traffic, would be the only way of providing on-street access to the city centre of Manchester.

A concept takes hold

After publication of the first report, GMPTE began a thorough consultation on the ideas with all ten metropolitan boroughs in the county and even adjoining district councils, and some of the RSG's observations were also adopted into the GMC County Structure Plan. This pragmatic approach to involving a wide range of organisations – even those which might not always agree – is seen as one of the main reasons why Greater Manchester has proceeded faster and further than any other UK region in developing modern light rail. David Tibke also suggests [19] that pedestrianisation (like that of Market Street in 1980 and St Anne's Square about the same time) and developments in light rail technology also helped to sway the RSG more favourably towards the possibilities of LRT for Manchester than might have been the case a decade or so earlier. Cllr. Andrew Fender suggested that politics played a key role too [20]: while Manchester City Council itself was heavily dominated by one party, Labour, the GMC had swung to Conservative control in 1977 (the first time this happened) and some of the Tory councillors also supported improving public transport infrastructure. In addition it just so happened that the Altrincham and Bury lines (with its ageing and potentially unsafe rolling stock), both terminated in areas which were under Conservative administration.

The strength of the light rail case was that improvements to the so-called Cinderella lines would bring economic and social benefits across the region and the political divide. Plus as Tibke says: "County cash was effectively being wasted on subsiding BR services which local councillors could not improve or control". [21]

RSG makes tracks

In order to better understand the benefits and problems of light rail in a busy city, GMPTE arranged a study tour during summer 1983 of nine different European systems. Nineteen representatives from the UK visited tram operations in Düsseldorf, Essen, Freiburg, Karlsruhe, Köln, Rastatt, Rotterdam, Utrecht and Zürich and a year later a smaller group from Manchester went to see the systems in Buffalo, Calgary, Edmonton, Portland, Toronto and Vancouver.

Tibke recalls that the deputation was met in Karlsruhe by enthusiastic local officials who were keen to show off their new trams – "so new that they were literally still in their factory wrappings". [22.] The Utrecht trams proved especially interesting to them as the configuration of the new light rail vehicles there matched that which the RSG perceived to be the ideal set up for Manchester,

Portland's vehicles are a hybrid between low and high floor.

given their high-floor access (plus, as historian David Holt points out, [23.] the orange livery of Utrecht trams was also uncannily similar to the colour of Greater Manchester's buses at that time). The RSG's first report was so influenced by these city visits that it included 60 pages describing them.

The second RSG publication in January 1984 was not shy about its favoured choice for the future of mass transit in Manchester: it was entitled Interim Report of the Preferred Strategy and featured on the cover a seductive artists impression (signed by: 'Albert Yeo') of a modern light rail vehicle on tracks turning between Market Street and Piccadilly Gardens. Citing the warm reception that the first report had received from those that were consulted and (perhaps more importantly) the Department for Transport, combined with the relatively rapid timescale in which construction could be undertaken, the RSG's firm recommendation was to proceed with the implementation of the LRT option. The RSG then boldly set about its third report, The Case for the Light Rapid Transit System, whilst GMPTE started the arduous task of preparing the first Bill for Parliament.

The first Bill

Legislation for the entire scheme was essential because not only were existing passenger railways to be 'closed' in preparation for conversion, but the task of placing new tracks in the public highway, and the effect that this would have on businesses and property adjacent to the construction is considered to be a matter of national law in the UK. It also allows an opportunity for those affected to object if they wish. So in November 1984 a highly detailed Private Bill was deposited in Parliament, which when passed would give the GMPTE powers to purchase land and begin work on the conversion of the commuter lines and construction of the on-street city-centre sections. Owing to the fact that no new tramways had been authorised in Britain since the 1940s, the Greater Manchester (Light Rail Transit System) Bill needed to refer

GMPTE's Tony Young was a regular guest explaining light rail benefits at BBC Greater Manchester Radio, here in 1987 with Natalie Anglesey.

(Above): Bus deregulation, here in 1987, caused a headache for the process.
(Opposite): 1988 rail diagram showing proposed light rail in colours.

to copious historic legislation going back as far as 1845. Tony Young recalls that: "partly as a PR exercise but mainly to create a mindset, Eric Black who later became Chief Executive of the company that operated the system insisted on the word 'tram' never being mentioned." [24.] It was so successfully expunged from the organisations involved that the word was barely uttered in Manchester for a good decade into the system's operation.

The most complex part of the task was always going to be the threading of the new on-street tracks through the centre of a crowded city. The route needed to be set out in the Bill with very little room for variation. From the south-western side, a relatively obvious, virtually straight-line trajectory existed between the end of the old Castlefield viaduct (by Deansgate station) and the side of Manchester Central (formerly the G-Mex exhibition centre and prior to that once Manchester Central Station), through St Peter's Square and down Mosley Street into Piccadilly Gardens.

Connecting between Victoria and Piccadilly stations however was the biggest challenge. As the crow flies it would have necessitated either a tunnel or a mammoth amount of demolition around Tib Street. Neither option would have brought the line that much closer to the existing commercial centre nor the city's largest bus interchanges. But to weave the tracks through Piccadilly Gardens (to give direct access to the buses) and even more tortuous, to push the tracks across Shude Hill to get into Victoria, involved great ingenuity. The technical prowess of the City Engineers proposals required the demolition of only a very short row of (ramshackle and rundown) buildings on Snow Hill: quite a feat. Detailed drawings for these central area tracks formed the lion's share of the Bill.

Second Bill, Assent and Money

The healthy dialogue and public debate around the scheme stirred up desires from the districts that would not benefit from the initial three-line system. Understandably local officials wanted to get their areas in on the act. The RSG's third report (November 1984) paved the way for the next piece of legislation that the complex process would require. The Department of Transport, though not hostile to the process, certainly threw down a number of obstacles. Their main concern according to Tony Young was that Manchester would "not do a Tyne & Wear Metro and try to construct the entire [6 section/3-line] network in one go". [25.] So the second Bill proposed that phase one would be the conversion of the suburban passenger line from Bury and the one from Altrincham which would be connected via the on-street section detailed in the first Bill. This was subsequently deposited with Parliament in November 1985 but because of delays and objections to the first more complex Bill, this second one effectively caught up with the first Bill lodged a year earlier. After all the objections were dealt with (and several landowners were paid off), both Bills achieved Royal Assent on 9th February 1988. As a salutary lesson to any later enthusiasts for light rail elsewhere, this date was the culmination of a four-year process. In the intervening period, bus deregulation had been passed and the GLC and the Metropolitan Counties (including the GMC) had been abolished by Government. The next Herculean task for the proponents of the scheme was to get the money to build it.

Apart from the obvious need to solve the problems of poor cross-city rail services outlined, one of the main reasons the RSG and its protagonists assumed they would be successful in obtaining some

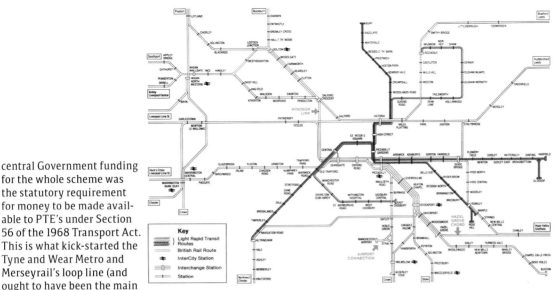

Key
- Light Rapid Transit Routes
- British Rail Route
- InterCity Station
- Interchange Station
- Station

central Government funding for the whole scheme was the statutory requirement for money to be made available to PTE's under Section 56 of the 1968 Transport Act. This is what kick-started the Tyne and Wear Metro and Merseyrail's loop line (and ought to have been the main pot for Picc-Vic. So in July 1985 GMPTE applied for a contribution towards the projected cost of £42.5 million of building Phase 1. Unfortunately the effects of bus deregulation in the 1985 Transport Act were unforeseen and threw out some of GMPTE's calculations made by consultant transport economist W.T. (Bill) Tyson of the cost/benefit analysis across different modes. Although the huge application document from Manchester would probably have satisfied all the previous criteria, the Department of Transport (DoT) was forced to issue new guidelines for Section 56 grants caused by the impending deregulation of all bus services (outside London) due to come into effect a year later in October 1986. One of the most infuriating aspects of the new 'free market' was that it would set bus services into direct competition with all other modes as opposed to facilitating better integration with bus services – the driving principle that had underpinned the successful funding of earlier projects like Tyne & Wear Metro.

Re-evaluation and Abolition

The Manchester grant application had to be completely re-calculated in response to the DoT's new guidelines, but GMPTE's experience in running bus services prior to their deregulation helped them to show an improved case for light rail. Meanwhile, the GMC, which had been such a driving force in the RSG and without whom the light rail scheme would have been dead in the water, had been abolished by Government by March 1986. Despite this disruptive blow, the joint body which replaced the GMC's brief, the Passenger

Transport Authority (PTA), confirmed its unanimous support for the light rail scheme. Nevertheless, despite having conducted their research, legal submissions and grant applications with impeccable professionalism in the face of major obstacles, including a Government that appeared to be more sympathetic to road building than railway expansion (it was later the instigators of the Serpell Report which almost brought about a second Beeching axe to the railways), Manchester was forced to wait another two years for any response to its application. During this time it transpired that as a result of new bus industry free-market, all other transport modes could not be given any 'unfair' advantage from public funded bodies. The Government's perceived intention then was ultimately to operate all public transport without subsidy, grace or favour.

The proposed Manchester operation would therefore need to be set up as a private company, competing for passengers on a 'level-playing-field' with bus and other modes. The belief in a free market economy went as far as the then Cabinet Minister and future train buff Michael Portillo declaring that most of the volumes of research submitted in the Bills would only ever be seen as "advisory" and would not need to be contractually binding upon the winners of bids to construct and run any system.

Tony Young said: "at this stage the government would have preferred the bills to be a single sheet of A4 saying roughly what was to be done, throwing out years of research into most effective manner in which to deliver the project". [26.] So the light rail lobbyists in Manchester set about a major publicity campaign to stir up support in the city and further afield. There was a promotional video, colourful leaflets, and in Gorton, a stretch of lightly used

Docklands P86 vehicle from London on a test track near Debdale, 1987.

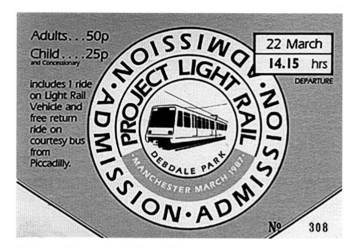

Admission ticket to ride the Light Rail Project, 1987.

freight line was given over for a three week exhibition called Project Light Rail, that turned out to be quite a legendary event.

Docklands in Gorton

On a chilly Tuesday morning in March 1987, GMPTE pulled off one of the most significant and visible stunts of their campaign: the Minister of State for Transport, David Mitchell, waved a red flag on a temporary wooden platform called 'Debdale Park' and a surprising second guest from the capital began its landmark northern journey. Breaking the tape for its first run on the 1.6km demonstrator track near Gorton was vehicle no 11, borrowed from London's brand new (yet even to officially open itself) Docklands Light Railway and adapted to run in 'driver mode', with a temporary pantograph collector fitted by GEC Transportation (whose headquarters were then in Trafford Park). Over the three weeks of the trial and accompanying exhibition and lectures about the future of Light Rail in Manchester, around 10,000 people visited the site and much excitement was generated: the BBC's local radio station, GMR, even ran a competition to name the future LRT vehicles.

Could it be that the city was finally to get the urban rapid transit system that it so badly needed? Well, not for a while at least. Whilst the wooden platform at Debdale Park had shown what the system could look like in a traditional railway environment (as it might

appear after the conversion of the old suburban lines to Bury and Altrincham), one crucial aspect of the trial that was missing was the chance to assess the feel of such an operation in a modern busy street setting.

High platforms & accessibility

The complexity of what GMPTE aimed to achieve with the design of the system should not be understated. What it was proposing had never been attempted in the UK before: although former BR lines had been converted to allow light rail vehicles to run on them (in Newcastle and London) no modern tram had been placed on British streets amongst general traffic. No stations or 'stops' had been built on UK roads, there were not even any suitable modern road signs in the Department of Transport's approved list. In addition, thanks to the fact that there was no money to lower the level of the existing high platforms on the Bury and Altrincham lines (35 of them), this forced the requirement to construct the city centre on-street platforms at an identical elevated height: something else that had never been attempted in the UK. In addition to all of this was a growing recognition of the needs of those with limited mobility. Manchester City Council (MCC), and some of the neighbouring boroughs had for some years been investing money and staff time in policy changes that would improve accessibility for those with restricted access.

1988 and 1990 leaflets promoting the coming system.

Mocked up fibre glass vehicle, Birchfields Road, 1989.

Building a new transport system from scratch meant that departments such as MCC's Equality Group (officers in the Chief Executives department) and other pressure groups were quick to call for the entire operation to be 'fully accessible' – so that it was suitable for anyone with mobility difficulties, ranging from wheelchair users to those travelling with prams or heavy luggage. The Equality Group estimated that at any one time up to 20% of the population could be suffering from impaired mobility, even if their limitations were not immediately obvious or visible.

The first place that the elevated street platform concept was displayed to the public was on a full-scale mock-up built in the Birchfields Road bus garage in the summer of 1988. Holt points out the irony of the location[27]: "...originally built as a tram depot as recently as July 1928 and sadly the destination of Manchester's ceremonial last tram on 10th January 1949." The faux platform and part of a proposed vehicle shell were left in situ until the winter as engineers and dignitaries from other systems around the world visited to fine-tune various specifications like railings and lights. There was no way that these high platforms could be built without providing easy access for the mobility impaired, so the idea of creating a gentle slope, or 'profiled-platform' was developed and displayed here. Despite attendance from the public being sparse, the small number of wheelchair and pram users reported that the 'gap' between the raised platform and the tram door entrance was

not noticeable: a testament to the clever work of the GMPTE and local architects EGS. However it was also apparent that the practicalities of creating high-level platforms in the city centre meant that in some instances there was insufficient space to build an access slope of the right inclination and also to have level access to the light rail vehicle along the whole of the platform – and even less practical with two vehicles linked together. This led to the flat access onto the vehicle being limited to a certain section of the tram and in other sections access was provided by a set of retractable steps. The development of these additional steps added to development time and cost of the vehicles, but it was still a more cost effective solution than buying what were at the time the more expensive low-floor trams and converting the 35 existing platforms on the former BR lines to accommodate low floor trams. Ultimately, access to certain platforms on the former BR lines had to be provided by lift as there was insufficient space for long ramps, another process that involved significant expense.

A public face and name

Up until this point the whole scheme was labouring under the slightly formal terminology of 'Light Rail Transit Project', and the word 'tram' was banned. But all transport systems need a catchy, and memorable moniker so an entirely new word was created when the name Metrolink was formally announced in June 1988.

(Above): Tony Young with school children making model Metrolink trams.
(Below): 1992 official Metrolink logo and colours, also used on livery.

Metrolink was also subsequently chosen in 1992 as the operating name for suburban commuter trains around Los Angeles, and was also adopted for the light rail system in St Louis, Missouri a year later. There was no logo for Manchester's Metrolink to begin with. GMPTE's logo, created in 1974 was a stylised letter 'M' referred to as a the 'double-M' (or less reverentially: the 'wiggly sausage') and as the system name began with an M it was this that was utilised for design mock ups and leaflets: but in the run up to the construction phase a proper logo was needed. The leading London design agency Fitch came up with a circular logo featuring a simplified M, rotated by 45 degrees It was very smart and used the latest colour graduated effects, but unfortunately the practical execution of this in print, on station signs and vehicle sides did not always work too

well. The logo was nicknamed "batman in a porthole" by staff due to its resemblance to a head with bat ears looking through a circular window. Station names (and the official typeface of Metrolink) were specified as Frutiger Black, although the word Metrolink was usually shown below the circular 'M' logo in capitals in a variant of Futura Bold. Occasional examples at Piccadilly Gardens and other city centre stops also show the system name in a light version of the Optima typeface – for

reasons that are unknown. As none of these typefaces were particularly common at the time, publicity material before and after the opening also appeared in a variety of typefaces, giving a somewhat incoherent look which took years to rectify. Later, in 1991 there was yet another public competition to come up with a snappier title, (a nickname like 'The Tube'). This was won by 'The Met', which has subsequently been adopted by (at least some) regular users. There was also a concerted effort to win over and inform the public about the forthcoming construction period, which even with the best will in the world was bound to cause some frustrations. As well as copious large signs erected around the city, plus newsletters and leaflets galore, a number of talks were delivered to schoolchildren, community associations and businesses.

Funding, private risk and 'DBOM'

After having jumped through so many hoops to make their application fit the latest Whitehall restraints, the acceptance in principle of Section 56 funding came in January 1988. "It has to be remembered that at this point in the Conservative Government, the concept of the free-market economy and the desire to restrict any unnecessary burden on the public finances was in the ascendancy" Councillor Fender told the author. So GMPTE was then forced to consider a variety of mechanisms that would move any long term funding burden into the private sector. The eventual scheme of 'Design, Build, Operate and Maintain' (DBOM) was effectively forced upon the GMPTE by the Treasury. This was a convoluted, and expensive process that ultimately was unlikely to save any tax payers' money at all, but the tendering process finally began with advertisements placed in the trade press during April 1988.

GMPTE were required to set up an operating company Greater Manchester Rapid Transport Company Limited (GMRT) and eight out of twelve consortia who applied to run it were whittled down to five (three withdrew) by the end of January 1989. These had been further reduced to three by mid-March 1989 for the second stage of

Utility relocation, Manchester City Centre, in late 1989.

Preparatory work in Market Street uncovered old tram tracks, 1990

the tendering process, but it was not until September of that year that the winning consortium of GMA was announced. GMA was made up of construction companies AMEC, John Mowlem & Co. and the engineering giant GEC. Finally after both GMPTE and the GMA had done yet more work on the costs for what was undoubtedly at that time the most complex financial structuring of any British transport project (only usurped by the intricacies of the London Underground Public Private Partnership, several years later), the Minister of State for Transport, Michael Portillo, announced on October 24th 1989 that Phase 1 of the Manchester Metrolink project would receive around £50 million from Central Government via the Section 56 grant.

The PTA was given permission by the DoT to borrow another £70 million from the Public Works Loan Board. The consortium itself added several million and yet more came from various channels and quangos (not least of which was a large contribution from the European Regional Development Fund).

In total the final cost of the Phase 1 scheme at 1990 prices was around £135 million. As many commentators have pointed out, the Picc-Vic tunnels (not including the other associated works) would have cost just over £9m at 1973 prices which would have been about £50m in 1990. The moral of the story is that it's always less expensive to do major infrastructure projects as early as possible! For legal reasons, yet another company had then to be formed for the implementation of the project which became known of as Greater Manchester Metro Limited (GMML). The enormous task of identi-

fying and diverting all the underground cables, drains and pipes from beneath the roads on which the tram tracks would be laid then commenced in 1989. More than twenty bus stands had to be permanently relocated, roads were temporarily closed and re-opened again – then promptly closed a few months later. The effects of the construction undoubtedly created significant disruption and had a major impact on mobility inside much of Manchester City Centre for several years. But construction was effectively under way.

Vehicles make history

Having got all the funding secured, the contractual side in order, utilities moved and visible track-laying work beginning in the city centre streets, attention turned back again to the light rail vehicles themselves. Given all the parameters needed for Manchester's on and off street operations, a company who could build the required fleet (in time and on budget) had already been located: they were the Firema Consortium, based in Italy.

Using at least 60% of materials sourced or manufactured in the UK, the 26 light rail vehicles ordered at a cost of £1 million each were to be assembled at various plants across Italy. A life-size pre-production mock-up was erected by GMPTE in 1990 beneath an old brick arch under Piccadilly station and accessed from an entrance on North Western Street (it now lives in the Greater Manchester Museum of Transport). Once fine tuning using this prototype had occurred, the first tram was ready in August of that year and was transported by land and sea across Europe to Manchester. When it

Jack Flannaghan, Chris Mulligan and Roger Hall, November 1991.

arrived at the newly built Queen's Road depot, the first in a fleet of T68 vehicles, car number 1001, made history by becoming the first new light rail vehicle designed for on-street operation to touch steel rails in the UK for at least four decades. Testing began almost immediately during which time the tram was towed along to ensure the gauging and other aspects were correct – numerous firsts and photo opportunities arose as the vehicle reached new parts of the city which had not seen a rail vehicle for so long.

The livery, produced by the originators of the Metrolink logo Fitch and the Cambridge-based transport design firm Design Triangle, featured a dark metallic grey for the window trimmings and lower 'skirt' with a lighter grey upper section. There was an aquamarine thin stripe running the length of the vehicle. The leaning 'M' circular logo sat on the line between the contrasting greys. The overall effect was very smart and clean – although there were always the inevitable grumbles that the grey was chosen to reflect Manchester skies!

British streets get first new track and poles for decades

The conversion of the two former BR lines to light rail use took major effort as they were so dilapidated, but aside from the track improvements (the old steel rails were kept), new signalling and power supply, and the provision of lifts and ramps where needed to improve accessibility, it was essentially more of a cosmetic and safety improvement operation. The placement of tram tracks on the road however was now such a specialised skill that the only people with any recent experience were in Blackpool, at the National Tramway Museum (in Crich, Derbyshire), or from overseas operators. The task was nowhere near as straightforward as building a normal railway: for a start there is no ballast piled in the streets so the tracks have to be held in place resting on a concrete bed under the road surface. The rails are different too: they have grooves in them. Vibration and noise are also issues in crowded urban areas

Building the viaduct down to street level beside the G-Mex, 1991.

Encased in 6000cubic metres of concrete, the undercroft felt subterranean.

and because the power supply return path is not supposed to escape from the rails they need to be electrically isolated. A specially prepared polymer was poured beside the metal rails to prevent current leakage and reduce vibrations. The rails also needed to be welded into a continuous whole. The Piccadilly Gardens triangular 'delta' required special attention and advice from the experience of the light rail operator in Portland, Oregon. The construction of the stops with their unique sloped ('profiled') platforms also had to be completed and they were equipped with standard furniture from JC Decaux and Ticket Vending Machines (TVMs). Lastly the modular signage system was erected featuring a similar colour scheme to the trams (dark grey background with aquamarine stripe) and white sans-serif text in Frutiger typeface.

The other taxing issue in the city-centre on-street section was the overhead wire and traction poles and the perceived intrusion into the streetscape that these might bring. Therefore intensive design work was undertaken to reduce the potential resulting 'clutter' in environmentally sensitive areas – for example running past the magnificent stone facade of the Art Gallery on Mosley Street. Here and wherever technically feasible, overhead wires were attached to the buildings themselves – reducing the need for so many traction wire holding poles. While this was partially achieved in the early 1990s, it was recognised that with more time and money spent assessing the requirements, fewer poles may have been needed. A number of poles have been removed in the intervening period.

Piccadilly: we have a problem!

As most of the other engineering progressed, a major problem arose with the proposed flagship interchange beneath Piccadilly main-line station. British Rail were concerned that in the event of an accident or fire the ancient 'undercroft' could be damaged causing potential structural issues with the massive weight of the huge terminal above. The problem was solved by project manager John Berry who suggested that instead of a single island platform there would be two separate faces with supporting iron pillars and the entire Metrolink station should be encased in a vast concrete box. Although this added several million pounds to the cost, it produced an effective and modern look which befitted the system.

The finishing was helped by grants from the Central Manchester Development Corporation (CMDC) and the result makes what is really a surface-level stop feel more like a deep underground one. Finally, after literally decades of false starts, years of planning and months of construction, on Monday 6th April 1992 at 6am, the UK's first modern light rail vehicle broke through the ceremonial tape at Bury Interchange station to enter public service.

Track laying beside Piccadilly bus stands, 1991.

Monday 6th April 1992 at Bury Interchange. An early start to service.

Piccadilly was the most expensive Metrolink stop to build and feels like a sleek, effective, modern transport hub.

(Opposite, bottom): 1002 passes the Town Hall in February 1992. (Above): Commemorative tickets for all the first days of service that took place in 1992.

Initially Metrolink only ran between Bury and Victoria (calling at Woodlands Road, Crumpsall, Bowker Vale, Heaton Park, Prestwich, Besses o' th' Barn, Whitefield and Radcliffe) but the first street-running section from Victoria to what was then G-Mex (via High Street, Market Street, Mosley Street and St Peter's Square) was opened a little afterwards on 27th April 1992. It is almost impossible to quantify the significance of the achieve-ment: not only did it herald the reappearance of trams on British streets (not to mention start the ball rolling for the growth of a network which significantly improved urban mass transit across the region), but the birth of the system gave a significant boost to the city's regeneration. The impact of Metrolink on wealth genera-tion, inward investment, civic pride and national standing is nigh-on incalculable.

Her Majesty the
Queen with
Councillor Jack
Flannaghan at the
official opening.

Openings fit for a Queen

One place where the significance of Metrolink was not lost was in
the run-up to the 1992 General Election: the Prime Minister of the
day, John Major, paid a visit to Manchester and was taken on a tram
and shown the future plans. Although his party won the election,
the trip did not seem to sway the Government over to funding more
light rail: a bid for Birmingham to build its first line was initially
turned down. The section to Altrincham was not able to be opened
until a little later, but on 15th June 1992, the Town Crier rang his
bell at the platform for the first light rail service to begin (calling at
Navigation Road, Timperley, Brooklands, Sale, Dane Road,
Stretford, Old Trafford and Trafford Bar). Then there was the small
matter of Royalty to accommodate for the grand official opening.
GMPTE pulled off a major coup in getting Her Majesty the Queen to
undertake the official opening on 17th July 1992. It was a magnificent event as recalled by tram driver Alan Walsh, who was introduced to Her Majesty before he drove the vehicle up to Bury with
the Queen on board. As he told reporters at the time "I'll never
forget the day when we set off in the July sunshine with the royal

personage on my tram." [28.] GMPTE's Bill Tyson, remembered that
"...it was odd because we'd been running the system for a few
months since the public opening, but I recall that on the day of the
Royal visit we had something like 50 staff on hand, just in case, and
we produced an entire book of instructions to help the day run
smoothly – which it did! It was a very proud moment for us
everyone involved to see it all come to fruition". [29.]

Getting under Piccadilly's skin

A few days after the Royal opening, on 20th July 1992, the last part of
this first phase to open to the public was the section from Piccadilly
Gardens down into the newly created concrete box beneath the mainline platforms of Piccadilly station.

The additional decor and smart finishing that was made possible by
what was essentially an entirely new build (albeit under century old
brick arches) produced a magnificent appearance. Piccadilly was head
and shoulders the landmark station of the new Metrolink system and
even had an underground feel about it, despite effectively being at the

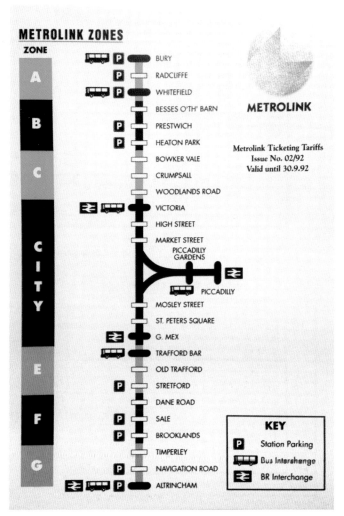

The second system map similar to those used on TVMs, late 1992.

same level as the street, from where it was accessed. It was also the only station to receive brand new escalators, and the ease of access to the mainline station above was undoubtedly a factor in Metrolink's early success.

Stops like Trafford Bar were unable to mask their former railway heritage.

The first phase was complete, providing 31 km of route with 25 stops. Maps of the system were issued in two styles: one showed the geographical trajectories more truly than the other: the portrait shaped diagram on the front of Ticket Vending Machines and used in most publicity had Bury at the top ('north') and Altrincham at the bottom ('south') but the in-car strip maps, much like those on the majority of the world's transit systems, were horizontal. This landscape format forced Bury to be placed to the right (looking somewhat easterly) and Altrincham, left (westerly).

Patronage in the first year exceeded expectations and by 1994 as officials began work on the second phase, the system was carrying 11 million people a year – 3 million more than the old rail services. All was boding well for light rail in Manchester, and the UK in general. But events in the rest of the coming decade were to change Metrolink's fortunes again.

"Parts of East Manchester
had become a huge swath of
dereliction embracing
almost 2,500 acres"
Professor Brian Robson, Manchester University

Regeneration Stations

By the 1980s virtually every port in Britain had succumbed to the pain of long term decline in manufacturing and exports. The vast expanse of inner city docklands beside the Manchester Ship Canal was no exception, but, through forward-thinking akin only to the expertise that revived similar derelict land along the Thames, work was afoot to revitalise an area to become known as Salford Quays.

The earliest new and refurbished buildings around Pomona didn't exactly hold much promise of the vitality to come later. Windswept, isolated and lacking in essential amenities, the first residents complained of poor public transport connections to Salford and Manchester. But GMPTE had signalled their intention to extend the Metrolink through the area from some of earliest light rail plans (1987). While this was not possible in the first tranche of construction, extensions to both Salford and Dumplington (later to be transformed into the Trafford Centre) were mentioned on the third light rail Bill and consequently allowance was made near Cornbrook during the first construction phase for a turn out which would later provide room for points and tracks to be placed in the direction of the land on both sides of the ship canal.

Phase 2: a different vision

By the early to mid-1990s when the first phase had proven itself a success, thoughts turned to expansion of the system. The first extensions envisaged were always more likely to have been on the eastern side of the conurbation (Oldham/Rochdale or even Marple/Glossop, which were also in the initial proposals from the RSG). Although it had appeared on long term plans for some years, taking any rail service into Salford Quays was considered by some to be uneconomic: after all the population was still almost nonexistent and there was little evidence that major workforce employers were on the way. The task of assessing the Salford extension fell to Tom Beaman (then working for GMPTE) who quickly spotted that the line would make more sense if it were to push on further from

Salford Quays development plan, 1989, included a Metrolink line concept.

Salford Quays into neighbouring, much more densely populated areas. After ruling out Swinton, Pendleton and Salford Precinct (among others), Beaman locked on a trajectory that would take the line north and west into the centre of Eccles, deep into the borough of Salford.

The problem was that after leaving the initial, mainly segregated, curvaceous route through the quays, most of Beaman's alignment would be almost entirely on street. Not only would this force some major engineering challenges as it would be entirely new build (i.e. not along any existing/former rail track bed) but the move into full on-street running in a suburban environment was completely new territory for Metrolink and had not really been foreseen in the preparation of earlier plans. Luckily, the Sheffield Supertram system (first opened in 1994) had been planned from the outset with much more on-street running than Manchester Metrolink, so there was less nervousness than there might otherwise have been about long runs down the middle of roads full of other traffic. Indeed following the success of Metrolink itself re-introducing light rail to Manchester, a large number of other proposals blossomed across Britain from Bristol to Glasgow: sadly the majority of these came to nothing.

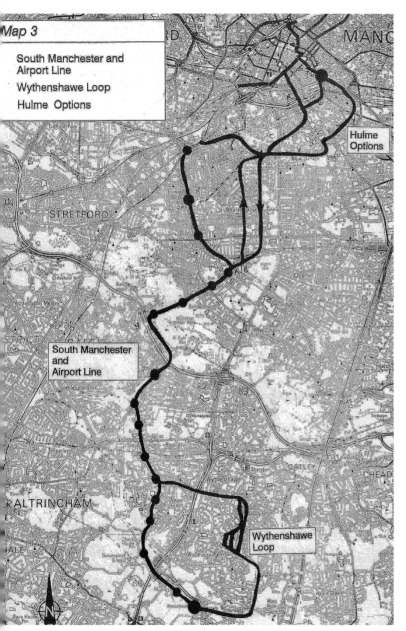

Map 3

South Manchester and
Airport Line

Wythenshawe Loop

Hulme Options

Hulme
Options

South Manchester
and
Airport Line

Wythenshawe
Loop

The switch to a more traditional European tramway mode though did mark a significant alteration for operations in Manchester and Beaman recalls that this was happening in the context of wider conversations about a European city model for Manchester at the time. The transformation of cities like Barcelona had given the leadership of Manchester City Council and the surrounding boroughs new ideas for the reinvention of the conurbation, one where a modern and efficient tram system had a major role to play.

A gap to be filled?

Inside GMPTE the opening of the first line was viewed with mixed reactions. Firstly, some people expressed surprise that they had actually 'pulled it off'. Others had concerns about how much it would get used. But the staff were fervently plotting the future. One extremely early deviation from the late 1980s ideas of only using old rail routes was an internal proposal to get light rail into Manchester Airport. There was also the thorny question of inner south Manchester which has been touted since the dawn of all mass transit schemes in the city as one of the most obvious trajectories ("a classic corridor for light rail," as Tony Young called it[30]). This was once one of the most intensively served parts of Britain by tram lines, built in the heyday of such services because of the high population located far from a suburban rail line. Of course, when the trams were removed and no new rail lines were built, inner south Manchester remained a dead zone for rail-based transport services.

All the 1960s schemes aimed to fill that gap, but they never materialised. Hence when the question arose of how to get trams to the airport, a series of alignments to bring the tracks through south Manchester called the 'Hulme Options' were examined before the cheaper alignments were selected of utilising the former rail bed to Chorlton. Although these ideas were discussed within the teams at GMPTE they have only recently come to light.

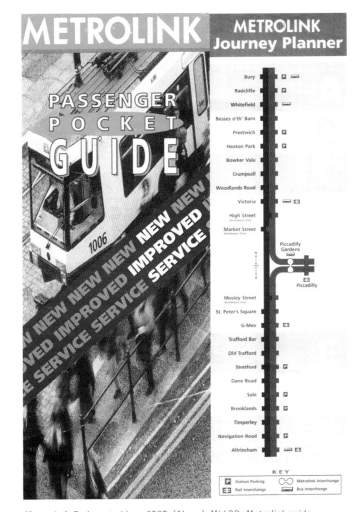

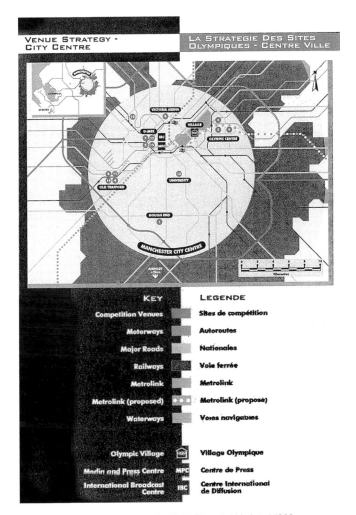

(Opposite): Early route ideas, 1992. (Above): Mid 90s Metrolink guide.

Proposed East Manchester route for 2000 Olympic bid, dated 1993.

Eccles gets its cake

Technical drawings were prepared in 1992 and public consultation on the route took place in 1993. Powers were gained by Parliament in 1995 confirming that Eccles would be served from the Salford Quays line. New trams would be needed for the fleet and GMPTE exercised their right to purchase more of the original T68s from Italy, with some braking refinements that rolling stock engineer David Beilby recalls were necessary. These six vehicles would be named T68As. A new consortium was set up to construct the 6.4km line. Christened Altram it consisted of the outsourcing specialist Serco, the Italian transportation company Anslado and UK

Pamphlets produced in the mid 1990s showed suggested routes, The 'Proposed stadium site' is what later became the Etihad stadium for Manchester City FC.

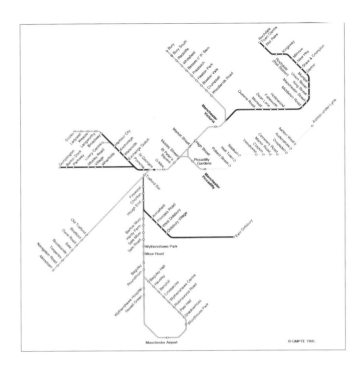

A 1995 GMPTE diagram showed remarkable foresight.

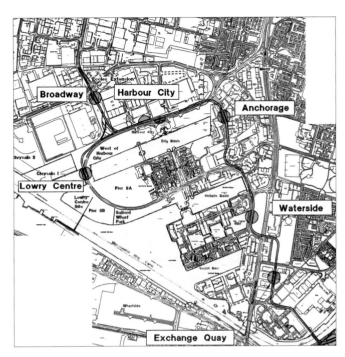

Early Salford Quays plans with branch to Lowry Centre.

construction giant John Laing plc. At the same time Serco took over the contract to operate and maintain the existing system. However construction of the route to Eccles did not begin until July 1997.

Bids bring big benefits

During the 1990s, the city of Manchester was involved in three bids for major sporting events. It first bid for the 1996 Olympic Games (which was won by Atlanta), got through to the third round for the 2000 Olympic Games (won by Sydney) and was finally awarded the right to stage the 2002 Commonwealth Games. The existence and benefits of the Metrolink system were highlighted in all three bids and it was seen as one of the city's biggest advantages over other candidates in securing the Commonwealth Games. By 1993, the official bid document for the 2000 Olympic Games contained a firm proposal to build a new Metrolink line to the planned venues which would be built on brownfield sites to the east of the city.

By the time of the bid for the 2002 Commonwealth Games (submitted in 1995), a proposal to extend Metrolink to the Airport was also fleshed out. The centrepiece of the earlier bids was Britain's first Olympic-standard velodrome. The main venue for the 2002 bid was to be the City of Manchester Stadium (which was subsequently taken over by Manchester City FC). It was proposed that these new facilities would be served by a new Metrolink line that would exit the undercroft of Piccadilly station and proceed eastwards, eventually leading to Ashton-under-Lyne town centre. Some preparatory work was undertaken early on: land and buildings were compulsorily purchased and most of the route to the stadium itself was cleared ready for the construction. But the process was held up by several events.

BR engineering work on the Hazel Grove chord had downgraded the imperative of converting lines to Marple and Glossop and the stalling of plans for the out-of-town shopping centre at

Part of the devastation caused by the 1996 IRA bomb. Although it was not foreseen at the time the trams would later run along here.

Dumplington (later to re-emerge as the Trafford Centre), forced a re-think on how a bigger network might look. Conversion of the original Oldham/Rochdale line was still on the table, but the concept of taking trams to Manchester Airport as well as eastwards to Ashton, via the event sites, got GMPTE brains whirring. What if they could build an entire network in one go? As early as 1994, the nascent concept was first named 'Metrolink 2000': it was mentioned in Parliament the following year and GMPTE began producing a whole series of promotional leaflets including fairly detailed maps which were issued to the public from around 1995.

Provisional work was also undertaken by GMPTE's Estates Department to purchase more land and buildings which might need to be demolished to make way for future tram stops (especially in East Manchester and Tameside). The brochures included diagrams of a new full network.

Metrolink
Linking the re-build & Victoria to Deansgate
How a new central route could integrate with existing lines and planned extensions. Plus possible extensions of the new route to serve Oxford Rd, Universities, Hospitals, Rusholme, Hulme, Moss Side.

A vision of the future from the IRA nightmare

By MARK OVENDEN

■ REVEALED below the Arndale Centre by the terrorist bomb are the remnants of a seventies plan to construct an underground railway link between Piccadilly and Victoria mainline stations enshrined in its subterranean roots.

Construction of the Picc-Vic line was stopped during the oil crisis and later attempts to link the two main termini were replaced by Metrolink.

Why don't we use part of these exposed early workings as the basis for a whole new extension to our tram system? Part of this would be underground, through the very heart of the devastation. It's an unparalleled opportunity for major urban regeneration.

Ideas for the lines' route include a starting point under Victoria station, where land is already earmarked for major development. The tunnels would then burrow straight towards the crater, making use of some of the abandoned platform works already in existence under the Arndale — almost exactly below where the bomb exploded. Here there would be a station with links directly into the reconstructed Arndale or whatever replaced it at surface level, plus access to the popular shopping areas of Shambles Square, the Corn Exchange and onto Corporation Street itself.

The route could then change course to tunnel below St Ann's Square ready for a stop on Deansgate.

From there, the route could be used to sweep round nearly all the proposed new developments in the city's upcoming north western quarter. Possible stop sites could include Granada Studios Tour, Castlefield, and the Science Museum, The Great Northern Development, and swing round for an interchange connection with the existing tram stop at St Peter's Square. From there, the obvious route would be to plough on down — or even surface up to run along Oxford Street and Oxford Road, possibly towards the highly populated Rusholme, Fallowfield and Withington areas. A branch heading for the renovated Hulme and Moss Side would be an obvious important addition.

What Manchester needs today as it looks at the ruins is a message of hope. The city prides itself on being the First, being the innovator — we must now look to the future with a bright, exciting, useful vision to pull from the city's worst nightmare a shining jewel.

© Mark Ovenden is a reader

Author's proposal of 22 June 1996 was among several published in the Manchester Evening News (map was not included in the original MEN article).

An explosive interruption

Preparations were getting underway for the new Metrolink line to Eccles, and the city was buzzing with anticipation for the European football championships being held in England at that time, when on a sunny Saturday morning on 15th June 1996 the Provisional IRA set off a massive 1,500k bomb in Manchester City Centre. Although there was a warning and 75,000 people had been evacuated, more than 200 were injured by what turned out to be the largest bomb on mainline Britain since WW2. A Metrolink tram was commandeered to ferry the injured to North Manchester General Hospital. Almost 50,000m² of retail space and 57,000m² of offices were put out of use affecting 400 businesses within half a mile of the blast. The enormous destruction caused by the bomb made the city even more determined than ever to pursue its regeneration agenda. While investment in the area was already well underway the need for

Stop locations in Salford Quays

(Above): Produced in late 1998, this GMPTE montage visualised how the Eccles line would weave through the Quays (lower left eventually became MediaCity).
(Below): In-car strip maps were updated to include the first Metrolink extension, with Bury-Altrincham in turquoise and the Eccles line taking a blue hue.

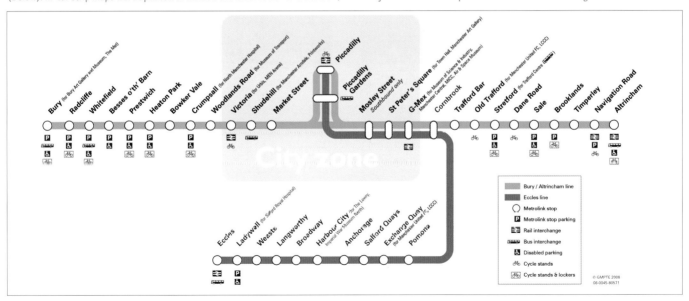

Prime Minster Tony Blair gives his thumbs up to the Eccles line.

Signage still used Frutiger Black plus the system logo: a nice touch.

rapid reconstruction of the city centre brought people, businesses and the public sector together, sparking new ideas and initiatives as well as creating a more positive attitude from central Government. With talk circulating of more Metrolink lines and services needing to cross the city centre, this author made a suggestion for a proposed 'second' crossing of the city centre to avoid 'tram-jam' when new services began. And while all these new ideas and concepts were being aired and debated, a new player, Serco Metrolink, took over the operations and maintenance of the system on 26th May 1997.

1997 computerised images of before and after at Pollard Street.

1997 computerised images of before and after at Ashton centre.

From the ashes

Meanwhile construction through Salford Quays by Altram (a subsidiary of Serco), which had begun in July 1997, progressed relatively quickly. The opportunity was taken to provide several new features for Metrolink: first of all there was an experimental area of track where grass trays were placed in between sleepers (an idea seen often on continental tram systems), and a new interchange station was built on the viaduct at Cornbrook (on what was previously a long uninterrupted run between the Trafford Bar stop and what was originally called G-Mex stop (and was later renamed as Deansgate-Castlefield).

1997 plan for Oldham Town centre involved a tunnel to King Street.

When Cornbrook first opened with the first phase of the new line (initially only Pomona, Exchange Quay, Salford Quays, Anchorage, Harbour City and Broadway) in December 1999, there was no access to the street as the area around it was relatively unpopulated. Britain's newly elected Prime Minister, Tony Blair presided over the event saying it was "exactly the type of scheme needed to solve the transport problems of the metropolitan areas of the country". But within a few years his Transport Secretary dashed the hopes of those determined to ensure Metrolink's further expansion.

Princess Royal for Eccles

The second part of the new line, almost entirely on street to Eccles (via Langworthy, Weaste, and Ladywell), was ready for passengers in July 2000 and its official opening was presided over by Her Royal Highness the Princess Royal on 9th January 2001. It represented the culmination of Metrolink's Phase 2 plans and even while the rails were still being welded, plans were already afoot to bring about the next and most ambitious phase to fruition. Peel Holdings' vast, out-of-town shopping centre, the Trafford Centre had been approved by 1995 and had opened its doors by September 1998, but at this point plans were advancing for the East Manchester line to serve the venues for the Commonwealth Games and a new line to service the growing Manchester Airport.

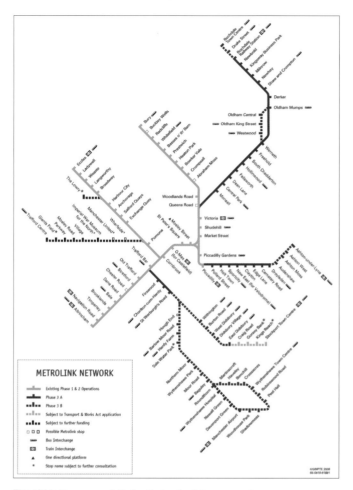

This 1999 diagram was full of optimism for future expansion.

A keen observer was regular Metrolink passenger and tram fan John McCarthy, who noticed some concrete track-bases heading into the unknown as the rails turned onto the Eccles line at Pomona. "I was fascinated: could that be the site of a future extension?" he told the author. [31.] But John and other passengers were going to have a long wait and a politically bumpy ride to see that future-proofed space being utilised.

(Above): Situated on a breezy viaduct, Cornbrook initially opened only for interchange to the Eccles line with no access to the street. (Right): Leaflets and maps like this gave an air of confidence that the expansions were happening – although this 1999 one shows yet to materialise Stockport plans.

Meantime 'Metrolink 2000' public meetings and consultations were happening across the region and new requests for lines to be considered for unserved areas were bubbling up at a rate of knots.

Stockport Metropolitan Borough were pressing to be connected to the burgeoning network and GMPTE updated its diagram of future lines to include it and a spur from the Eccles line to the Lowry Centre.

By 1999 the plans all seemed so achievable. The only obstacle in the way was getting the money released from Government and, with its leader having gone on record about what a beacon for regional transport the Metrolink system had become, surely nothing could stop the expansion of Metrolink now? The 2000s were about to test that belief to the full.

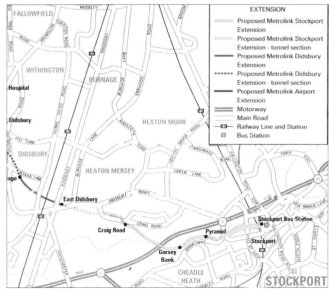

EXTENSION

Proposed Metrolink Stockport Extension
Proposed Metrolink Stockport Extension - tunnel section
Proposed Metrolink Didsbury Extension
Proposed Metrolink Didsbury Extension - tunnel section
Proposed Metrolink Airport Extension
Motorway
Main Road
Railway Line and Station
Bus Station

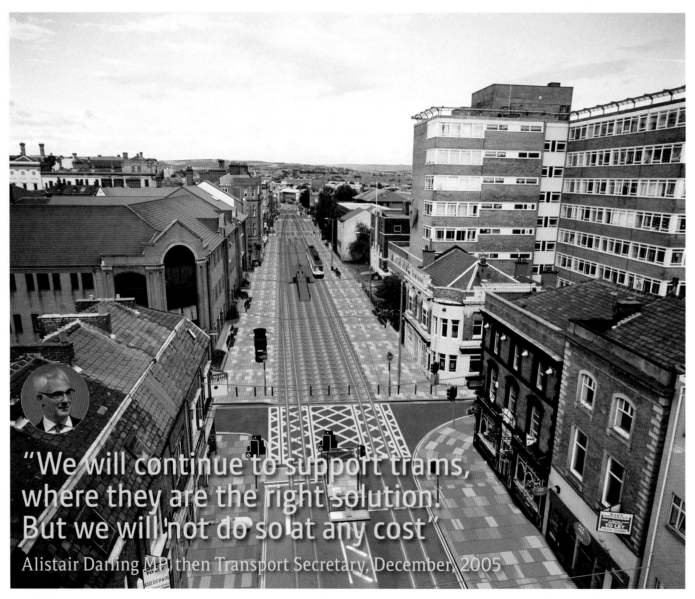

"We will continue to support trams, where they are the right solution. But we will not do so at any cost"

Alistair Darling MP, then Transport Secretary, December, 2005

Computer visualisation of trams on Union Street. The Oldham Town centre section fell victim to the Government's initial withdrawal of funding.

Big-Bang (in Theory)

Tram extensions vanquished then vindicated

As has been seen, Manchester's role in the renaissance of building tram systems in the UK was absolutely pivotal: not only was it the first of a tranche of modern light rail schemes, but it had well-developed aspirations for a full network, right from the outset. Although the precise trajectory of some routes had evolved over the years, the impetus of events, and the popularity of the system, had led GMPTE to be hopeful of gaining the funding they needed to build all the proposed extensions in one go.

Meantime, small incremental improvements were still happening across the existing network. The city centre has seen the greatest number of alterations to the stops: for example the one-direction platforms at both High Street and Market Street were merged into a single island platform stop in 1998 when the pedestrianisation of Market Street created the spaces for this to happen. Taking advantage of the need to relocate a bus station from under the Arndale Centre to a plot of land adjacent to the Metrolink tracks in Shudehill, GMPTE commissioned Ian Simpson Architects (now Simpson Haugh) in 2000 to draw up plans to provide a new tram stop in order to make it into a tram/bus interchange. The new Metrolink stop opened on 31st March 2003, although the bus station itself was not ready until 2006.

Audit changes everything

The "Metrolink 2000" project had jumped all the hurdles from public consultations to gaining the parliamentary powers necessary. They were submitted to the Department of Transport (DoT) for funding in 2000 which coincided with submissions for brand new light rail schemes in West Yorkshire (Leeds Supertram) and Portsmouth (South Hampshire Rapid Transit). There was high optimism that these applications would progress without any obstacles after all, the DoT indicated in March 2000 that "funding was available to support up to 25 new light rail schemes". [32.] All three were

The Shudehill in-fill stop created a new bus/tram interchange.

initially approved to get the money they required (Manchester by July of that year and the other two by March 2001). In December 2002, the Secretary of State for Transport, Alistair Darling MP had stoked the flames of hope further by praising Metrolink and stating in Parliament: "I can confirm today funding approval for three new lines, which should more than double the number of passengers carried. Construction is planned to start next year". [33.] Darling even opened Nottingham's new light rail line NET in April 2004.

The original cost predicted in 2000 for Manchester's extensions was £282 million but for a number of reasons prices had escalated substantially during the period when various consortia were asked to bid to deliver the work. In May 2003, the DoT informed the proponents of all three proposed schemes (Manchester's extensions and the new networks for Leeds and South Hampshire) that

The GMPTE headquarters on Piccadilly swathed in campaign banners.

they were concerned about rising costs. There was an additional complication in Leeds because a proposal had circulated that a Bus Rapid Transit scheme would be better value for money. By 2004 the amount required to build the Manchester extensions (including buying a new fleet of light rail vehicles) had increased to over half a billion pounds and the cost of the other schemes had also risen. The last remaining hurdle in the way of the schemes' approval was HM Treasury, and they suddenly got cold feet.

No little darling

Despite the nervousness stirred up by cost increases, no-one expected what would happen next: Councillor Roger Jones (then chair of the Passenger Transport Authority, GMPTA) recalled the day of a Parliamentary announcement (Tuesday 20th July 2004) to the author: "I had been informed that the Secretary of State for Transport would be making a statement which would include refer-

ence to Metrolink. I whizzed down to the House of Commons to listen to the statement assuming that Alistair Darling was going to finally approve the £520 million we needed. I was hoping to organise a celebration when I got back to Manchester. When he announced that he was unable to approve the schemes I was completely staggered and I immediately met a number of Greater Manchester MPs in the Commons, including Graham Stringer, Keith Bradley, Jim Dobbin, Ian Stewart, Lorna Fitzsimons, Phil Woolas and David Hayes. We basically agreed that they would arrange a meeting with Prime Minister Tony Blair and we would all support a co-ordinated campaign [to reverse the decision]. My first job was to rally the troops back in Manchester." [34.]

The north fights back

The shock was greeted with understandable anger and frustration in Manchester. There was a palpable feeling (even if factually incorrect) that while money seemed to be forever available for transport schemes in London (the Crossrail project was looking like it would

A T68 tram covered in campaign material, 2004.

be funded – and later was), anything outside the capital faced repeated hurdles and setbacks. Echoes of the Picc-Vic cancellation from three decades earlier haunted GMPTE and the city seemed to unite against what was perceived as an unnecessarily harsh and unjust decision.

Local media (not always the biggest supporters historically of Metrolink), but especially the Manchester Evening News, rallied around and a campaign entitled "Get Our Metrolink Back On Track" launched on 12th August 2004. It rapidly gained huge momentum. A rally was held on 2nd September in Tameside, one of the areas to be served by the extensions, followed four days later by the launch of a campaign tram and two days after that a huge banner was erected on the GMPTE offices (45m wide and 7m high). Further rallies were held in Oldham, Rochdale and Manchester in September and a series of fringe meetings were put on at all the major party conferences during September and October. Prime Minister Blair and Darling himself met a group of Greater Manchester MPs on 15th September and this led the PM to set up a special working party in October with Transport Minister Tony McNulty, Keith Bradley MP, Chris Mulligan, then Director General of GMPTE and Penny Boothman from Manchester City Council.

Other events captured the collective imagination: a train full of members of the public, business community representatives and the media travelled to London on 10th November. Roger Jones took a coach-load of schoolchildren and the actress Jennie McAlpine (Fiz from Coronation Street) to 10 Downing Street "We met Gerald Kaufman MP and delivered 41,500 messages of support for the Metrolink extensions". [35.] By December 2004 the campaigning work seemed to be paying off: things were getting back on track. Jones met Darling in Manchester and they travelled on the Metrolink together before a meeting at the Town Hall. Darling even conceded that the July announcement was not one of his best decisions but he was worried about rising costs. Finally on 16th December Darling announced that £520 million would after all be given to Manchester Metrolink extensions, but: "subject to an agreed plan".

The campaign bus at Edge Lane in Droylsden, 2004.

A tiff over the TIF

In order to access the money that Darling had then said they could have, Manchester had to jump through a number of hoops. The first of which was a somewhat complex new method for any English authority to access public money to invest in transport: the Transport Innovation Fund (TIF). Created in July 2004, the fund was supposed to open up almost £10 billion to be allocated to local schemes over seven years. But the catch was that applicants had to demonstrate their proposals would take cars off the road. The PTA and the Association of Greater Manchester Authorities (AGMA) decided in 2005 to bid for a large slice of the fund with a smorgasbord of transport improvements, which would include funding for all the Metrolink extensions and money to improve and maintain the existing fleet of trams.

A smaller bang but not a whimper

The Darling deal was in some ways quite clever, but with hindsight it also became a bit of a false economy. In an act of fairly typically Mancunian pragmatism, the protagonists' idea was to make a start on what had come to be known of as the 'Big Bang' batch of extensions, but because prices had gone up in real terms and no new money was available, it would be possible to partially complete

METROLINK NETWORK

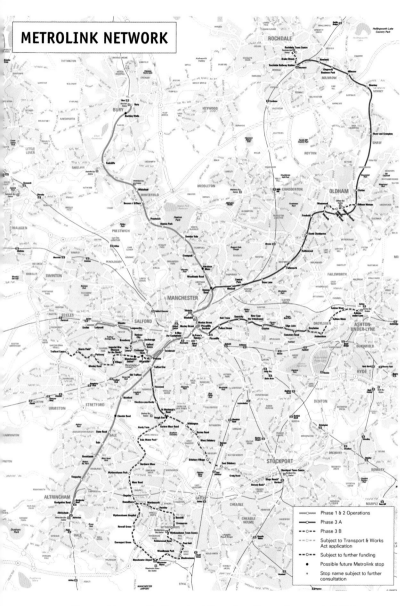

Geographic map of both parts of Phase 3 and beyond as seen in 2007.

The campaign was worn around the city on T-Shirts and placards alike.

them. Officially renamed as Phase 3a (and colloquially as 'Big Bang's Little Bang') the work would involve a start on three lines but each would suffer some curtailments from the full proposals:

• **Oldham and Rochdale line**, (a.k.a. the ORL), originated from the 1980s aspiration to convert the existing BR commuter line to light rail. Over the years transport planners had understood the limitations of these older routes (this one dating from the mid 1800s) many with their stations on the outskirts of what became the central areas of towns. So the full scheme was to create new sections of light rail directly into the commercial centres of both Oldham and Rochdale. Tracks would slew off the older lines and run on street into the heart of each town. Inevitably these two diversions were some of the most expensive parts of the engineering: so the cut-down Phase 3a proposal would utilise only the old trackbed and both town centre extensions would have to wait for more funding at a later date.

• **East Manchester line** – the EML. Despite land having been compulsorily purchased and the demolition of homes to make way for the trams to run all the way into Ashton town centre, Phase 3a would only be able to take the tracks as far as Droylsden.

• **South Manchester line** – the SML. Another remnant from the 1980s proposals, this line utilised the long-closed Manchester South District Railway between Trafford and Didsbury. At certain

Central Park (and the bridge in the background) sat in the wilderness with no track for some years.

continue to cite a Metrolink extension into the borough as a very high priority.

The bid for funding for the newly formulated and slightly curtailed 'Phase 3a' became part of an Integrated Transport Strategy (ITS) which was submitted to the Government on 8th April 2005. The first batch of money was released on 30th June that year to pay for urgently needed track improvements on the Bury line and the purchase of the first eight of the new trams.

points in the planning, this route had been mooted to forge down into Stockport but the curtailed route for Phase 3a was to take it only as far as Chorlton's St Werburgh's Road.

• **New Trams.** It was envisaged that 50 new trams would be needed to service the entire Phase 3 project but since it was going to be built in stages the initial order was reduced to 28.

• **New depot.** A new depot was always understood to be required as the original one at Queens Road would not be able to house an entirely new fleet. Also having two depots one on either side of the central area is a wise move to ensure network resilience. No significant changes were proposed to the depot plans for Phase 3a.

Other losses from 3a

• **Airport line** – the MAL. This had to be dropped from Phase 3a, as was the full continuation of the loop to serve Wythenshawe Hospital, which would have run from the Airport northwards, back to Roundthorn. It was seen as the least potentially viable section of the route and was removed from Phase 3a and indeed the subsequent 3b.

• **Stockport** – despite much lobbying, this was also due to be an expensive section to construct (due mainly to the Motorway crossing) and has so far been eliminated from current plans. Hopes are still high for it to be added in the future and the local authority

A park with no ride

Despite Darling's announcement and in the heat of the campaign to reverse it, a bold statement was happening in East Manchester. In anticipation of the conversion of the Oldham/Rochdale line, architectural plans were being drawn up for a brand new station, provisionally to be called North Manchester Business Park (although later renamed Central Park) and construction work began in September 2005.

The move was considered a wise one by GMPTE to make an early start on this one station as it was to be at the heart of an urban renewal project called The Gateway and close to the proposed new headquarters building for Greater Manchester Police, which duly opened in 2011 housing more than 1000 staff.

With its striking curved glass and copper roof designed by architects Aukett Fitzroy Robinson, the Metrolink stop has been affectionately nicknamed by some as 'Pringle Henge', but while work on the structure was completed rapidly, the trackbed remained empty...for seven long years. The unconnected station however became a symbol of the pause in Metrolink expansion caused by the funding crisis, and later a beacon of its success.

Darling looking decidedly uncomfortable when visiting Metrolink.

Cornbrook to street

The interchange-only stop at Cornbrook had never been designed to be accessible from the street, mainly as there was little residential development in the area. But stairs had been made for use in emergency and as new apartments were constructed nearby, demand increased. Following £250,000 worth of improvements, Cornbrook was converted for full access from the road below and opened as a proper stop with street-access on 3rd September 2005.

Darling drops in, then out

The Secretary of State for Transport, Alistair Darling, visited Manchester on 21st October 2005 to discuss the city region's transport vision for the next 15 years. It is fair to say he must have felt the tension in the atmosphere (he was jeered by members of the

public on several occasions) but transport officials acted with huge professionalism. Not long after the visit, he was replaced as Transport Secretary by Douglas Alexander, who in July of 2006 finally approved the two stage expansion. The curtailed Phase 3a would be followed at a later date by Phase 3b (theoretically to be funded by new money from a different pot). Whilst the official go-ahead for 3a was greeted with unparalleled relief in Manchester, it was also tinged with great frustration that the lines would all be terminating short of their intended destinations. One of the most unfortunate losses of 3a was the somewhat odd situation it would force upon the line in Oldham.

Improvements down the track

One of the first visible new items from the July money was to be the replacement of the original Ticket Vending Machines (TVMs) with new ones that would be capable of accepting other methods of payment like contactless and smart cards. Another would be the provision of eight new, wider trams. This package of improvements to the network was agreed by Government on 15th September 2006. Two months later there was also a grant of almost £2m provided by Government to allow GMPTE to examine all the options for bidding for the TIF money and funding the Phase 3b line extensions. In the same month Carillion Construction was appointed to replace about 20 miles of worn out track on the original routes: GMPTE's Interim Director

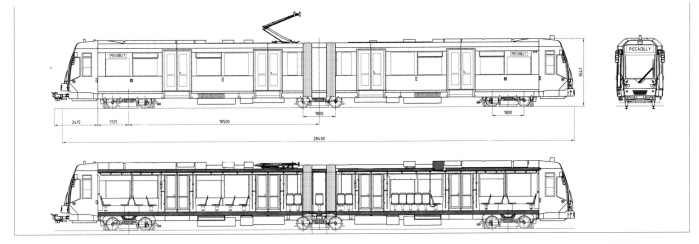

(Opposite, bottom): 2006 mock-up of what MediaCity plaza might look like complete with tramway. (Above): Technical drawing of the proposed M5000.

General at the time, David Leather, said: "The track on the Bury and Altrincham lines is more than 50 years old in some places and is rapidly approaching the end of its natural life".

Bid of a TIF, bit of demolition

By the summer of 2007 the revised bid for TIF money was ready. It coincided with Stagecoach taking over as the Metrolink operator.

The Bombardier/Vossloh Kiepe K5000 in Bonn.

On 27th July 2007 the Association of Greater Manchester Authorities (AGMA) decided to submit a bid of £3 billion to the Government's Transport Innovation Fund (TIF). This enormous sum was for a huge shopping list of transport funding (the largest outside London) with the promise that a road congestion charging system would be introduced in Manchester. The plans were not just for the Metrolink expansion but also for things like longer trains, high quality bus services, Park and Ride and Yellow School Buses.

Rejected livery and logo for Metrolink.

The first M5000 gets fitted out at the factory in Austria.

Road charging revenue would be retained for funding public transport improvements in Greater Manchester. In order to deliver all the already approved (and hoped for future) extensions, GMPTE appointed Parsons Brinckerhoff to ensure they were built on time and budget.

A landmark event happened on 23rd October 2007 though: a garage in Clayton was demolished. Not at face value a monumental act, but it was the first of five derelict buildings to be cleared for the start of the new Phase 3a Metrolink line to Droylsden. In the same month, planning permission was finally granted for the 360 metre spur off the Eccles line to serve the development that been re-named MediaCity:UK

Originally planned as a route towards the Lowry Centre, the trajectory was slightly altered to place the platforms immediately in front of a cluster of new build that would form the northern home of the BBC when it moved from its old studios on Oxford Road in the city centre. Four new trams were also ordered to serve the line which would branch off at Harbour City to run into the new plaza.

New tram, new era

The T68 trams which had served Manchester since the opening of the system in 1992 were looking a bit tired fifteen years later – and anyway the production line that made them in Italy had long since been broken up. With the approval of a major expansion and the full size of the network expected to need over 100 light rail vehicles, the decision was taken to look for a brand new design of tram for Manchester for the initial eight that were needed immediately and for those that would be required in the future. By the 2000s low-floor vehicles had become all the rage and thousands of them had been built and were operating around the world. They were inevitably also a good deal cheaper than when the Metrolink system was being established. But it was clear that it would not be possible to jump ship and switch to low-floor trams for the city as

Rejected theme for stations and trams by Steer Davies Gleave, 2007.

Hemisphere/Design Triangle livery concept for the M5000, 2008.

the walls at Victoria station". [36.] The refinements needed for the Manchester model were still being designed into early 2008 but by the September of that year when Beilby visited the plant he witnessed the cabs being manufactured and he recalls: "By early 2009 the first body shells were being placed on the bones and by the end of March it started to look like a tram. Testing happened in the company's Vienna plant and they even opened a new factory in early 2008 to make them in (not just the Manchester ones – they were also becoming one of the world's most popular family of light rail vehicle)".

the entire existing operation was set up to accommodate high-floor vehicles. The only problem was that there were now far fewer manufacturers making them.

Luckily for Manchester several European cities (Rotterdam, Bursa and Cologne/Bonn) were still using a high-floor design: the Flexity Swift model built by the Canadian company Bombardier in partnership with Vossloh Kiepe. The company had also built several low-floor versions (for example those used on London's Croydon Tramlink) and their K5000 (named after Koln) was just the ticket for the Manchester system. After some negotiations, GMPTE made a provisional order for the first eight new vehicles at a cost of £17m in April 2007 – with the proviso that they would order 28 more for the start of Phase 3a operation later.

The new vehicle would be known as the M5000. GMPTE Rolling stock engineer David Beilby recalls visiting the Bombardier production factory in Germany: Beilby told the author: "The 5000s were a good fit for Manchester. The vehicle size was ideal for our tracks and their 'sweep envelope' was almost spot on for the positioning of the existing traction poles in city centre and key elements like

The semiotics of reliability

To mark the massive investment in Metrolink, GMPTE Committee members felt it essential that a new look was devised for the network as a statement about this step change in Metrolink's development and their ambitions for its future. But the pressing requirement was to develop a new livery for the trams as the M5000s were

Sue Vanden and Grant Windridge of Hemisphere.

MetroSans - ASCII Set: 2008-10-24

| Metro Yellow | Metro Silver | Metro Bronze |
| PMS: 122C/120U | PMS: 877C | PMS: 8003C |

(Top): Bruno Maag's Pantograph notes. (Above) The initial logo. (Right): Hemipshere's colours. (Opposite): First new signage placement at Piccadilly.

due to roll off the production line in Vienna and the base colour of the vehicles had to be decided as a matter of urgency.

Manchester had recently taken the innovative step of appointing a Creative Director for the city, selecting the renowned graphic designer Peter Saville for the role. Working with the Manchester-based branding agency Hemisphere, Peter developed his own theories about how the new Metrolink trams should not just look, but how they should feel. Sue Vanden from Hemisphere takes up the

story: "We had interrogated a lot of the customer research that existed about Metrolink and one of the things that people really complained about was the reliability of the old T68s – they were perceived to be always breaking down. Our discussions with Peter focused around what he termed 'the semiotics of reliability' i.e. what makes an Audi feel more solid and reliable than a Toyota? His view was that we had to give the new M5000s a real feeling of solidity. They also had to have a feeling of aspiration – if ultimately what we need to do is to persuade BMW drivers to leave their cars at

PICCADILLY
It's an Undercroft!

Before and after photos of Piccadilly station stop show just what a difference the bright, clean yellow signage and smart new typeface made to the ambiance in this crucial circulating environment.

home and use public transport, then making the trams feel elegant and very European was key to achieving that goal."

Hemisphere and Saville agreed on a base silver colour for the tram and identified that an added nose colour and graphic treatment of the tram was necessary to make them highly visible, particularly as they moved at street level through busy pedestrian areas such as Piccadilly Gardens. According to Creative Director, Grant Windridge, Hemisphere arrived at yellow by a process of elimina-

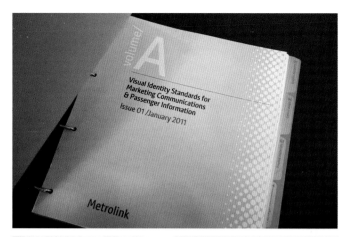

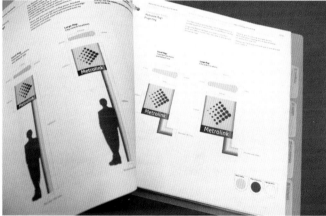

(Above & Right): Pages from the Hemipshere agency's Visual Identity Standards for Marketing, Communication & Passenger Information.

tion "In a city like Manchester using either red or blue is a non-starter. Purples don't stand out very much in the built environment and neither do greens, so we focused on selecting the right colour of yellow – the 'colour of optimism' – to work with the silver base."

"We deliberated long and hard about the exact colour of yellow, with Peter even texting me a picture of a yellow VW polo he spotted on a side street during a trip to Scotland! We all wanted to avoid the acidity of the hazard/warning yellow and arrive at something more

The LINK

The state-of-the art tram stop at Central Park on the Oldham and Rochdale line has already been built

Metrolink gets green light

Work to build three new tram lines in Greater Manchester is due to start early next year after transport bosses shook hands on a multi-million pound deal.

The Department for Transport has given the final seal of approval for a £575 million expansion of the Metrolink network – nearly doubling its size.

The new lines will run to Oldham and Rochdale, Droylsden and Chorlton, opening up new links to work and leisure for thousands more people across Greater Manchester. The new services are due to be up and running between 2011 and 2012.

The three new Metrolink lines are expected to take five million car journeys off local roads every year, and to increase the number of trips passengers make on the network each day from 55,000 to more than 90,000.

Philip Purdy, Metrolink Director at Greater Manchester Passenger Transport Executive (GMPTE), said: "People across the region have supported the plans to expand the Metrolink network. Without their backing we wouldn't be in this position today.

"Without their backing we wouldn't be in this position today"

Transport Secretary Ruth Kelly MP

"The new lines will cover nearly twenty miles and take the tram network into three new districts – Oldham, Rochdale and Tameside – as well as into South Manchester.

"Metrolink has helped to make Greater Manchester a vibrant place to live and work, and has been incredibly successful in other parts of Greater Manchester. I'm pleased more people will now be able to benefit from it."

The government is providing nearly £250 million for the Metrolink expansion. The rest of the money is being raised locally.

Transport Secretary Ruth Kelly said: "Metrolink has been at the heart of Greater Manchester's transport system for more than a decade.

"These much-anticipated improvements will make a huge difference to local public transport. Giving final approval to these plans reflects the government's commitment to providing convenient, reliable and comfortable public transport."

This encouraging publicity leaflet from 2008 was one of the last items produced by GMPTE in the old typeface and style.

(Above & Below): the overgrown former railway to Chorlton, 2008.

(Below): Equally forlorn: abandoned track bed near Monsall (2005).

sophisticated and classy whilst still maintaining the necessary contrast levels to satisfy the Rail Accessibility Regulations"

Alongside reliability, another key aspect from the customer research was speed – getting where they wanted to go quickly. Hemisphere created the 'speed graphic' pattern for the side of the trams and developed a computer-generated model of the newly-liveried M5000 at the new Shudehill tram stop. Approval was given by GMPTE development committee and the new M5000 was born. "The external livery of the tram was the immediate requirement but the new colour scheme would have ramifications across the network if Metrolink was to have a coherent future brand identity.

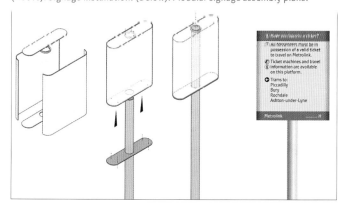

(Above): Signage installation. (Below): Modular signage assembly plans.

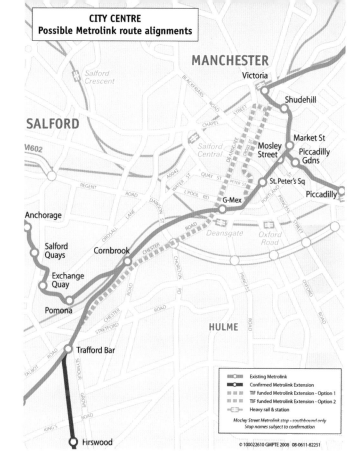

Two proposed alignments for a new crossing of the city centre, 2008.

Types of the times

To develop the livery design into a full-fledged identity for Metrolink, Hemisphere and Saville agreed the need for a singular typeface that could do for Metrolink what the Johnston typeface had done for London Underground and eventually for TfL as a whole.

With support from the GMPTE internal design team, Hemisphere made the case for commissioning the much-respected font foundry Dalton Maag to develop a new typeface for Metrolink, with the longer-term goal of applying it to all aspects of GMPTE's work. The font had to be highly accessible to be suitable for signage but also highly-distinctive so that people would instinctively associate it with Metrolink and GMPTE.

One of the first diagrams to include the proposed Second City Crossing, this one from 2008 being produced for the £3 billion TIF fund bid.

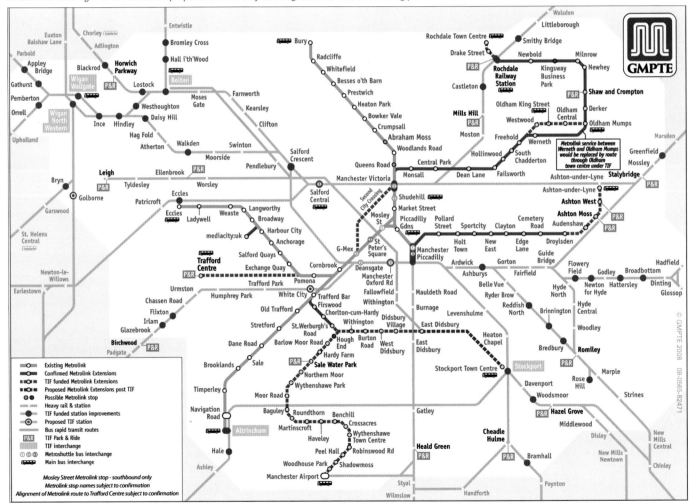

A former railway signal on the closed Chorlton suburban line in 2008 was about to see more than water run past this spot in the coming years.

According to Dalton Maag's Director, Bruno Maag, "99% of transport operations use sans-serifs for their signage (London Underground's Johnston being the first in 1916). But Hemisphere persuaded us to create something a bit different for Manchester. By introducing a small element of varied widths for the letter terminals, we effectively created a hybrid between a traditional san-serif and a blocky serif typeface". GMPTE approved the final version in 2008 with the recommended name of Pantograph. With the beginnings of a colour scheme and a typeface agreed, Hemisphere then set about devising a new signage scheme for Metrolink using the Piccadilly stop in the undercroft as its first testing ground.

Piccadilly gets the treatment

Windridge recalls: "..what we were aiming to create was the feeling that if you were travelling on Metrolink you could be on any light rail system in any European capital city. The old signage was pretty terrible: dark, gloomy and actually not very helpful, so we put ourselves in the shoes of a visitor to the city, or someone with mobility difficulties and tried to do a proper way-finding system from the bottom up. Access to every platform was considered so that people who couldn't use stairs were clearly signposted to the lifts and directional and service Information was clearly visible."

Work began in 2009 and although the new modular signage system was more expensive it had enough flexibility that it could be updated as the system expanded, giving it greater longevity. The transformation of Piccadilly made a significant impression: it was instantly distinctive, smart and modern and immediately lifted the ambience of the upgraded stop. At last Manchester seemed to enter the twenty-first century and was ready for the start of major expansion of its light rail network.

"That's why we proposed the unique new typeface for everything which the operator would own and be distinctively Metrolink" concluded Windridge.

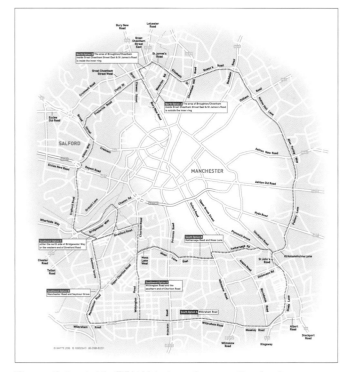

The map that sealed the TIF bid fate: inner ring congestion charging.

A bit of a tram jam (as predicted)

As anticipated by many commentators and professionals alike, if all the proposed extensions were finally to materialise, the city centre section could potentially become so busy that it reached capacity. By the end of 2007 this concern coalesced inside GMPTE with the idea to provide another route across the city centre which bypassed the busy Mosley Street/Piccadilly Gardens corridor. Two options were brought forward (from several other possibilities that were analysed): one that would bring the tracks to street level before the long Cornbrook viaduct and enter the central area from Chester Road, passing along Deansgate and joining back onto the existing tracks at Victoria.

The alternative route would be for the tracks to exit after the viaduct drops to street level (beside the Manchester Central

Work starting on the abandoned Smedley Viaduct, December 2009.

Convention Complex) and wind around Mount Street into Cross Street passing right along Corporation Street and into Victoria. At least three intermediate stops were envisaged for the Deansgate route and two for the Cross Street one.

The proposals for what was then called the 'Second City Crossing' were put out to public consultation in June 2011, with the majority favouring the Deansgate option as it would potentially bring more of the city centre closer to a tram stop (for example the rapidly expanding Spinningfields area). However that route was not to be, as will be seen later in the story.

Trafford Borough leaflet on the TIF referendum.

(Above). Queens Road depot would be too small for the new fleet.

(Below): MediaCity takes shape in 2008/9.

Gearing up for 3a

During the first half of 2008 several more key milestones were achieved in the run-up to the 3a construction works. Engineering manager Jim Harries, who oversaw the construction of Metrolink Phase 1, returned to Manchester in April to help organise Phase 3a. At the same time GMPTE picked the M-Pact Thales consortium as their preferred bidder for the 'Design, Construct and Maintain' contract of 3a but the PTE were also required to return to the Department for Transport for final sign-off on the project. In May GMPTE appointed a new Director: Australian Philip Purdy from Melbourne who then witnessed the final sign-off of Phase 3a by then Transport Secretary Ruth Kelly. By June, it was realised that the total number of trams on order would rise to 28. The tram bodies were already in production and the new livery was unveiled

Bombardier's Peter McNeill and Markus Dorlöchter of Vossloh-Kiepe examine the cab of the first M5000 at the Vienna factory, 2009.

The full 3b

Designing the look of the system, and even the development work on ideas for the second city crossing paled into insignificance compared to the intricacies of the TIF bid. A 2008 diagram showed the existing rail and Metrolink network with the 3b sections in dotted orange (including an imprecise trajectory of the proposed Second City Crossing, the Airport line, Oldham and Rochdale town centre routes and Trafford Park line), plus two dedicated bus priority routes. The map also included mention of the extension from East Didsbury to Stockport as 'post TIF', and the bid was chock full of dedicated cycle routes, improved interchange hubs plus an electronic smartcard that would be Manchester's equivalent

M5000 gets its first street test in Vienna, autumn 2009.

publicly during summer 2008: at the ceremony Grant Windridge, Hemisphere's Creative Director, said: "Our aim has been to create a bright and iconic tram that is easily recognisable on the streets. We chose yellow not just because of its high visibility but also because its traditional association with confidence and optimism echoes Greater Manchester's attitude and values." [39.]

Clearance work had also begun on the South Manchester line: another important achievement because this was the section of railway closed to passengers under the 1960s Beeching cuts. Tram fans like John McCarthy were keen to document the progress as what had become more of a water way than a railway was gradually cleared of vegetation and drained from an area near to Trafford Bar (firstly) to what became the St Werburgh's Road stop. Meanwhile GMPTE engineers were already out surveying and examining other parts of the proposed routes across Greater Manchester. Also, the Disability Design Reference Group (DDRG) was established by TfGM in 2008 to ensure that accessibility for passengers was fully embedded in the entire Metrolink expansion and enhancement project.

The first of the new trams with livery arrives by road, 16th December 2009.

of London's Oystercard. The Government even approved the package in June 2008. But approval and actually releasing money from the Whitehall coffers is no easy task.

For a start there would be the slightly awkward and never before attempted issue of a local referendum to ask if people across the Greater Manchester conurbation would be willing to pay a charge to drive in the congested areas of central Manchester and Salford. Campaigners on both sides went into overdrive and much publicity was produced by the local authorities and GMPTE.

The main thrust of the argument – to receive £3 billion of investment in improving public transport across the city region – was summed up by GMPTE under a campaign entitled: 'GM Future Transport'. Their documents triumphantly proclaimed the result: "will undoubtedly be the most far-reaching and transformational urban transport investment and change programme ever embarked upon in the UK outside of London". [40.] Maps were issued and confidence was high.

TIF Referendum says no

To pay or not to pay: that was the question, but the problem was that people do not usually vote for higher taxes (especially in the run up to Christmas).

The referendum to decide on whether or not to begin a Congestion Charge in Greater Manchester was lost by quite a large margin as 79% of those who voted preferred to avoid a congestion charge and not get access to the additional funding – a clear case of jam today rather than jam tomorrow. The outcome was that the TIF bid had to be rejected and the Association of Greater Manchester Authorities formally abandoned the entire bid on 19th December 2008.

3003 has a chilly start for one of its first runs, December 21st 2009.

Two of the first batch of new M5000s in service at the newly refurbished Piccadilly Gardens stop in 2010.

New year, new starts

At the end of that year though engineering inspections began on the former Smedley Viaduct. At 30 metres high and 400 metres long the 26 arches were last crossed by passenger trains in 1966. The overgrown vegetation had already been cleared in November but now work could begin in earnest to make the structure safe and prepared for the forthcoming construction works on the line towards Oldham and Rochdale.

Meanwhile in Vienna, Manchester's new trams were taking shape and work had begun on installing the electrical and interior fittings to the shells. And back in Droylsden, by February 2009, utilities like gas, water, electricity and phone lines were being diverted

The first official schematic for in car strip maps and TVMs in the new format and typeface, produced towards the end of 2009.

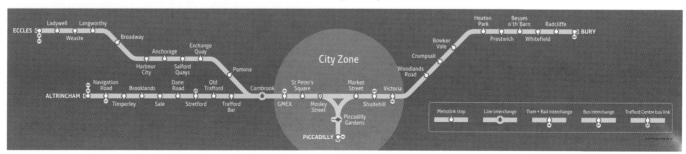

Clearance, site preparation and build of the new Trafford depot.

away from the route of the forthcoming new tram line on the street. They were exciting times in the region, despite the loss of the referendum vote.

Greater Manchester Passenger Transport Authority (GMPTA) became Greater Manchester Integrated Transport Authority (GMITA) on Monday 9th February as a prelude to further changes in the way the city region would be run, which in turn would lead to great strides forward for public transport, as will be seen.

Trams need homes

The original Queen's Road Metrolink depot needed expansion to cope with the forthcoming extensions. Work began on this project in April 2009. The maintenance workshop would be extended and additional stabling sidings were to be built. In addition a brand new depot was needed on the south side of the network and the last remaining derelict building on the second depot site – a former bakery and packaging company west of Trafford Bar stop – was

(Below): old and new signage side by side, 2010. (Above) the refit of Piccadilly stop, the first to be done, in yellow signage, 2010.

demolished during January 2009. Subsequently most of the ground had been cleared of old surfaces. By May 2009 it was also possible to begin full construction work on the short spur to MediaCity:UK. At the same time drainage was to be installed along the South Manchester line. This was to be followed by piling work later in the year on concrete foundations of the new tram stops. Philip Purdy, then GMPTE's Metrolink Director, said: "Once the drainage is in place we can start building the stops, so people are going to be seeing lots of activity on the line to Chorlton over the summer."

Wrenching victory from the jaws of defeat

Having failed to secure public support for Congestion Charging, and hence the £3 billion for improving transport, a new plan arose. On 13th May 2009, AGMA created a Greater Manchester Transport

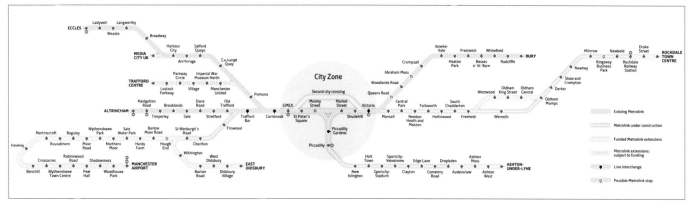

The 2010 schematic of all planned and funded extensions shows just how much work had been done to rescue the lion's share of Phase 3b.

Fund (GMTF) prioritising public transport and highway schemes. It proposed to pay for most of the outstanding Metrolink extensions (to Manchester Airport, East Didsbury, Ashton-under-Lyne and the town centres of Oldham and Rochdale), as well as the second city crossing between Victoria and the now renamed Deansgate-Castlefield stop. Transport Secretary Geoff Hoon welcomed this fast-tracking approach to the long awaited work. Meanwhile construction was underway on the route up to the Central Park station that had been completed several years earlier and had stood as a beacon for getting the extensions back on track. One of the reasons why the Metrolink could not use the entire route of the old

Oldham/Rochdale line into Victoria is that it would have entered the terminus on the wrong side of the station. So the plan had always been to deviate from the old BR line after it left Dean Lane and hop over the existing tracks on to a new bridge to take up another abandoned rail alignment on the Smedley viaduct. This would enable trams to run into Victoria (with the Bury ones, joining them at the Irk Valley junction) on the correct side of the busy station. M-Pact Thales, the consortium appointed to design, build and maintain the new lines, had already cleared the route and began installing drainage in June. The concrete foundations for the remaining tram stops began to be placed after that.

Following guidelines by the Hemisphere agency, TfGM's Simon Platt designed this schematic of the existing system in 2010, assigning colours to lines.

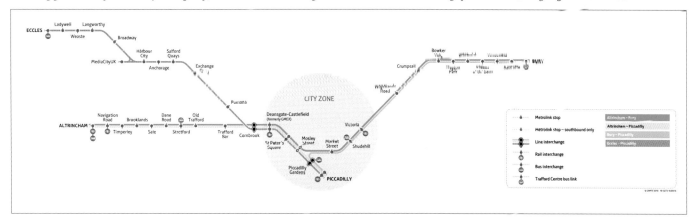

CHANGING CHORLTON

Progress on the South Manchester line was fairly brisk: (Top left) shown first as an overgrown relic of the Beeching cuts days, approx 2007. (Top right) In winter 2009 kids look over the parapet to see vegetation clearance under way. (Bottom left) by summer 2010 tracks and concrete platforms bases are in. (Bottom right) Just before overhead is strung up, the platforms already have some canopies and track is ready.

Queens Road receives a special delivery

After months in design and build, at the massive Vossloh-Kiepe Vienna factory and test track, an exciting birth was delivered to Manchester on 13th July 2009: the first new Metrolink M5000 tram arrived on a low-loader with a police escort by road at 6am. It was the first one to travel the 1000 miles through Germany, and the

Netherlands, crossing the sea from Rotterdam to Hull. The new vehicle with its yellow front end and metallic silver sides already had the graded dot Metrolink identity applied (subsequent trams had this section added in the Manchester workshops). The new colours also featured on the interiors where the seats were covered in a hard-wearing moquette.

When the first vehicle arrived it needed to be thoroughly tested as it was a completely new design on British streets and track: it was required to complete 1000 miles of endurance tests before it would later be allowed into service, and even after that all the drivers would need their training, so it did not get used by the travelling public until December 2009 when it entered service between Piccadilly and Eccles.

Cross Street, cross choice?

During August 2009, GMPTE forwarded their business case for the second crossing of the city centre to the Department of Transport. The route which ended up being chosen was not the longer one along Chester Road and Deansgate but the shorter alternative along Cross Street. This did cause some frustration among local businesses and residents as they claimed that it would not help in bringing a stop any closer to their area, but it was the cheaper option and also GMPTE had concerns about having trams running on another major road artery through the city centre. A small local campaign was formed to encourage the PTE to change its mind and route the trams along Deansgate by dropping the tracks down from the viaduct near to the Beetham Tower, but it transpired that engi-

Tram enthusiasts did a great job of documenting the progress too. These are from the South Manchester line at the temporary terminus, St Werburgh's Road.

Pushing out east from beneath the Piccadilly station, 2010

New lifts (here at Etihad Campus), crucial to give level access for all.

neers had examined this possibility before suggesting the Chester Road section, and dropping the tracks down from such a great height and turning a corner at the same time would have proved technically difficult and probably much more expensive. So Cross Street became the preferred option with the planned two intermediate stops reduced to one: to be at Exchange Square.

Two stops more Bury line stops and progress down south

There also came news that funding had become available for two new stops that would be opened on the Bury line: Queen's Road, location of a tiny staff-only "halt" designed for the depot workers, would be expanded into a full stop to serve the housing nearby, and the Woodlands Road stop which was always felt to be poorly located, would be moved to a new site and renamed Abraham Moss

– better serving a community centre there and with improved access to more residents.

Towards the middle of December there were some fitting finales to a decade which had seen high hopes for Metrolink expansion, some major setbacks and then finally the start of massive construction. Work began on preparations for the next extension of the South Manchester line from its temporary terminus at St Werburgh's Road (not yet opened, but where the build was well advanced) to the future terminus at East Didsbury. As some of the vegetation on this long overgrown section of old railway was blocking the route, particularly in leafy Chorlton, GMPTE had promised (as it had elsewhere) that for every tree removed, many more would be planted in its place. This was another promise kept. By the end of the Big Bang some 93,000 trees had been planted.

First outing for new trams

On 21st December 2009, after months of trials and driver training, the first M5000 light rail vehicle which had arrived earlier in the year, entered passenger service for the first time. Councillor Keith Whitmore said that "Passengers will notice the difference on the new trams" and promised: "it will be a smoother journey by far, with none of that 'clickety-click' of the old worn out track". 2009 saw a rash of closures for repairs as GMPTE undertook essential upgrades to the system to prepare it for the twenty-first century.

By this point 40 new trams had been ordered, and they were getting widespread support. Pete Waterman, veteran record producer and rail enthusiast, said of them on launch day: "The new trams are great, they're quite light, simple, they look bright and

In typical Mancunian style: a long section of open space was reserved for years in advance for the future arrival of Metrolink. Here at Shadowmoss, 2010.

European, and that's smashing to see in Manchester: it brings Europe closer and makes the city look more modern".

Refit or bust

Now that the new livery was starting to appear on the trams and works were well advanced for the Phase 3a extensions, the rolling out of the new station style and upgrading of the old stops came in

Laying of the first of the two tracks in Droylsden, 2010

to full swing. Not only was it important to replace worn-out lifts at places like Timperley, Brooklands, Sale and Dane Road, but the much needed redecoration of existing stations to match the proposed look of the new ones was well underway. With the new signage approach trialled at Piccadilly Gardens deemed a success, Hemisphere set about creating a comprehensive set of signage guidelines that were used to implement the new look at existing stops on the Altrincham, Bury and Eccles lines. This also included applying the brand to the new shelters that were due to be installed at refurbished city centre stops such as Piccadilly and Market Street. GMPTE's internal graphics team took up the mantle of implementing the new look for the new stops being built for the 3a extensions, as Louise Shaw, GMPTE's Design Manager recalls: "That period of around 2008-2010 leading up to the opening of the

New lift shafts and signage awaiting the opening at Firswood, 2011

One of Oldham's landmarks just before demolition..

new stops was absolutely electric: we were constantly providing the architects with drawings for how to apply the graphics standards to new stations, and when we saw them emerge it was so thrilling".

Milestones

Despite the setback the year before, all the parties had been working behind the scenes to bring about some alternative methods of funding the full desired Metrolink expansion programme. Three major milestones were reached in the first half of 2010: on 5th March GMITA's Capital Projects Committee released £26 million to fund design and preparatory work on the Airport line. At 14.5km from St Werburgh's Road to a new stop beside the existing mainline rail station in the airport, it was to be the longest piece of new build (i.e. not on old railway alignments) so needed a lot of preparatory surveying including environmental studies.

Three days later funding for the section from St Werburgh's to East Didsbury and from Droylsden to Ashton town centre were also approved by the Government. The total costs were £170m which allowed an order to be placed for a further eight new M5000 trams. Although the Department for Transport contribution was limited to £121m – and 6 vehicles – the rest was to be found locally. GMPTE's cartographer, Simon Platt, had the challenging task of constantly updating the Metrolink system map to show both its current and future state, as the different funding elements dropped into place.

There needed to be a few changes to save money though: for example on the Oldham/Rochdale route. Towards the end of that month, Oldham was informed that there would no longer be the planned stop at Werneth. The bridges and elevated section of the former BR track across the roundabout at Mumps (near a new temporary station that would have to be built) would be demol-ished. Phase 3a would then run at ground level all the way. It was also shown that for Phase 3b, instead of building any tunnels which were in the original proposals, Manchester Street roundabout would also be at ground level but with signal-controlled level cross-ings. In the vicinity of the hilly area near the former Pennine hotel, the line would be in a cutting.

The tunnelled section beneath Alan Turing Way in East Manchester had been made at the same time as Central Park was built so it was tested relatively early.

(Top left): Coronation Street opening titles added a tram in 2010. (Top right & below): A "Politanlink" tram crashes off a viaduct into the set, December 2010.

The 3b Mumps stop would end up beside the former B & Q store which with a Park and Ride area would provide a tram/bus/car interchange. The Phase 3a route through the old rail tunnels to Mumps station would close when Phase 3b opened in 2014 – becoming Metrolink's shortest-lived section of track ever.

No soft soaping for Corrie

The ITV soap-opera Coronation Street probably needs no introduction, but for anyone who has not seen the programme it is Britain's longest running and most popular TV drama. When the opening titles were updated to HD in May 2010 they included a tram running across the viaduct: reflecting the fact that the system was reaching right across Greater Manchester, even to the fictional suburb of Weatherfield. Trams featured in the script on many occasions but for the culmination of the 50th anniversary edition of the programme later in 2010 a huge explosion was planned in a bar (The Joinery): to be followed by a tram careering off the damaged viaduct above and crashing firstly into a corner shop, killing the characters Ashley Peacock (Steven Arnold) and Molly Dobbs (Vicky Binns), then into The Kabin, trapping Rita (Barbara Knox). The mocked-up tram vehicle resembled a T68 Metrolink-esque yellow livery (and even the 'go-faster' dots), but in order to distance itself from the official system and aid its setting in Weatherfield, it was branded as 'Politanlink' and numbered 1030 (which had never existed in the real fleet). Whilst transport operators are not thrilled to have their vehicles – even fictional ones – involved in anything negative, it was of course, all good exposure for Metrolink. And, as trams clearly do not generally plough through brick walls, it was all taken with a pinch of salt by the operator and the audience alike. The live show was watched by almost 15 million viewers.

New government: new direction

With the election of a coalition government in June 2010, a few sceptics thought that might be the end of the tram expansion

M5000 trams on test at St Werburgh's Road, 2011.

programme. There was however a bit of hope in the documents released in the run up to the election: "We will reform the way decisions are made on which transport projects to prioritise, so that the benefits of low carbon proposals (including light rail schemes) are fully recognised". [42.] Just after the result was in and the coalition formed, the Chief Secretary to the Treasury announced a public spending review but it did not include mention of the Greater Manchester Transport Fund. The Department for Transport then informed GMPTE that the East Didsbury and Ashton Metrolink extensions will not be affected so they should continue as planned. In fact from the point of view of devolving power to the regions, the city found itself in a surprising lead over other provincial centres – with supporters in very high places.

Before the election month was out, the new depot at Trafford had been completed, installing all the stabling yards and mini platforms for maintenance and cleaners. The overhead line was electrified too. On the other side of the city, the £10.5m expansion and modernisation of the original depot at Queen's Road was opened on

Early birds waiting for the first tram from St Werburgh's Rd, 2011.

15th July 2010 by the new Transport Minister, Norman Baker. It meant that it could now house 44 trams, and with the fleet growing from 30 to 80, more space was self-evidently greatly needed.

Around the same time there were more milestones on the South Manchester line: tracklaying for the full length of it was completed, as were construction works for its three stops (Firswood, Chorlton and the temporary terminus at St Werburgh's Road). These works were finished in break-neck time: both outbound and inbound tracks had been laid to the full length of this section by early July and the foundations of the stops was advancing. Lift shafts were being installed at Firswood stop and the start of work on traction poles had begun.

Getting to heart of Oldham and Rochdale

The GMITA and AGMA approved funding (and even had contracts signed) by the end of July for the expansion into both Rochdale and Oldham town centres and for the long Airport line. This meant that half a billion pounds had come through the Greater Manchester Transport Fund: a monumental amount for a transport project outside the capital. M-Pact Thales (MPT) were appointed to design, construct and maintain the new lines and the construction was due to roll on from when the Phase 3a work was completed. And it

didn't take long for clearance work to begin at the roundabout by Oldham Mumps: the original old railway had run over two bridges and a viaduct but all three had to go to allow Metrolink to penetrate the town properly. The viaduct in particular had achieved a certain amount of notoriety by the painted advert displayed on it for decades: stating 'Oldham: home of the Tubular Bandage'. A somewhat dubious claim to fame, but one which had become loved by the locals for its quirkiness.

The idea was that by removing these three structures the light rail tracks would be at ground level. So in early August the preparatory work to remove the viaduct and bridges began and over the Bank Holiday weekend, one was demolished by being cut up and lifted away. The stone viaduct went over the next couple months.

One of the short-lived T68 trams wrapped in the new livery.

Driver training at South Chadderton, 2012.

G-Mex renamed and MediaCity:UK opens

The Metrolink stop situated next to Manchester's huge conference centre had been called G-Mex (after the original name for the exhibition hall) ever since the system opened, despite the venue's name changing to Manchester Central in 2006. It was finally renamed on 20th September 2010 to more accurately reflect the stop's geographic location: Deansgate–Castlefield. As it was on the same date that the new spur to MediaCity:UK was opened to the public; the opportunity was taken to replace maps and signage to reflect both. MediaCity was the first new stop to open from scratch with the Hemisphere branding which was a perfect location as it seemed to echo the bright new skyscrapers alongside it. Timetabling services to MediaCity:UK – which was the first 'offshoot' route that Metrolink had operated – took a little while to settle down and with the services used by many hundreds of workers at both the BBC and ITV Studios, there were undoubtedly some initial hiccups before a stable service pattern was achieved.

Checking Chorlton and raising Rochdale

The first testing along the Chorlton extension took place in November 2010. Both the older (T68) and new (M5000) models were manoeuvred gingerly along the brand new rails from the (also brand new) depot at Old Trafford to the (also brand new) temporary terminus at St Werburgh's Road. The trams were not able to run under their own power as the overhead line was not yet ready, but both vehicles passed their gauging tests as they travelled past the other new stops at Firswood and Chorlton. The lines were energised to both the depot and the South Manchester line on 19th November. As the New Year began a flyover to lift the Metrolink over the Leeds-Manchester mainline railway started construction between the two existing bridges over Milnrow Road. It was a hefty project, requiring a 1000 tonne lift and 400 tonnes of steel. The southern bridge at Oldham Mumps also required heavy lifting: it was removed at the end of January 2011. RATP Dev took over operational management of the system from 2011.

Modern trams complementing the new offices at MediaCity:UK

(Below) Tram testing near New Islington, early 2013. (Above) Clayton Hall on the line to Droylsden in January 2013 as a tram passes under test conditions.

More power to Manchester

Given that it was the Conservative Government that had abolished metropolitan authorities (like the GMC), it came as a surprise to some that George Osborne, Conservative MP for Tatton, became the driving force behind the idea of devolving powers away from Whitehall that would help to deliver a concept called the 'Northern Powerhouse'. The inaugural meeting of the newly-created Greater Manchester Combined Authority (GMCA) took place on Friday 1st April 2011. Its establishment would prove pivotal in the process of devolution and new powers for the city region which would allow it to expand and fund Metrolink still further. Three days later, the first meeting of its Transport for Greater Manchester Committee (TfGMC) took place with representatives of the GMCA and the ten district authorities of Greater Manchester. The TfGMC was to take on responsibilities previously undertaken by the GMITA, advising the GMCA on transport policy. More publicly, GMPTE would also change its name to Transport for Greater Manchester (TfGM). The committee also delivered its Local Transport Plan for the next 15 years, in which Metrolink featured prominently.

Summer of Abraham Moss, Chorlton and Rochdale love

After a quick build, the new stop on the Bury line for Abraham Moss opened on 18th April 2011. Woodlands Road, just 250 metres away, would eventually close. But the big news of the summer was the July opening of the South Manchester Metrolink line. It brought fast journey time to Chorlton residents with trams taking just 15 minutes to run up to St Peter's Square. And in the same month several changes were enacted for the long spur into Rochdale town centre that would help it avoid a five-month delay (and substantial costs). The original proposals had been for double track along Drake Street into the new terminus, Rochdale Town Centre, beside the existing bus station, but engineers discovered that major structural

(Below): Outside Derker the line runs through open country, with the Pennines behind. (Above): The single track section dropping into Rochdale Railway Station.

(Below): Test tram entering the tunnel at Didsbury Village, 2013. (Above): Tram on test passing Kingsway Business Park stop, 2013.

work would be needed to take the lines across an old bridge over the River Roch. The double-track was therefore reduced to single track over the problem area before returning to two tracks on the approach to the terminus. Plans were also approved for a stop at Rochdale's regeneration area, Kingsway Business Park.

T68s for early retirement and early start for Oldham

As the rebrand of the stops was underway and the new M5000s were becoming a regular sight on the street, an attempt was made to try to apply the yellow and silver branding onto the older trams, the T68s. The result was not entirely satisfactory, but it wasn't this that caused TfGMC to order 12 extra M5000s to accelerate the replacement of the original T68s: they were now becoming so unreliable that it was cheaper to retire them early. After extensive testing and a week of ghost running, the first tram bound for all stops to Oldham Mumps left Victoria at 05:24 on 13th June 2012. It marked another significant milestone for the system and added 12km to the network. After Monsall the next stop out of Victoria was the once 'white-elephant' structure at Central Park. Inveterate tram watcher John McCarthy said: "The foresight of planners building this stop long before it was finally served acted as a lightning rod for anger over cancellation of the expansion and is now a flagship for what will become Britain's most extensive light rail system". [43.] Next stops were Newton Heath and Moston, Failsworth, Hollinwood, South Chadderton, Freehold and Westwood, for which the line offers much more frequent services than were previously available when it was a British Rail branch and is yet more proof that crumbling and unreliable BR branches can have new life breathed back into them by conversion to light rail. Meanwhile work on the remaining section of the line towards Rochdale continued apace. Testing happened in October 2012 when a tram crossed the Mumps roundabout at street level for the first time. The proposal was to get line open as far as Shaw & Crompton early in 2013 with the section to Rochdale Railway Station to follow within months.

Dynamic Droylsden, Motorway crossings and more openings

A few miles south of all the action in Oldham, exciting developments were taking place in East Manchester: under cover of darkness on 9th October 2012, the first tram ran to Droylsden and back – with a Police escort! Drivers were then trained (in daylight) and testing carried on into the New Year. Early the following month, (even further south), two motorways needed bridging for the new line to the Airport: the M60 and the M56. The design of these new bridges was so clever that the installation of each one only required the respective motorways to be closed for a few hours.

On 16th December 2012 the Oldham line service was extended to Shaw & Crompton (with an intermediate stop at Derker) and test trams were already up and running between Shaw and Crompton and Rochdale Railway Station by early the next year. Just as Peter Cushing took over as the new Director of Metrolink. Cushing presided over the opening on 12th February 2013 of the East Manchester line from Piccadilly to its temporary terminus at Droylsden (via New Islington, Holt Town, Etihad Campus, Velopark,

Clayton Hall, Edge Lane and Cemetery Road). By this date, local residents had already benefited from three days of free local tram travel as a thank you to for putting up with the disruption of the construction work. John McCarthy was among them: "..this was such a brilliant few days, I heard my neighbours suddenly speaking positively about the possibility of using the tram after putting up with quite extensive periods of disruption from the works. It was great to hear". [44.] Just a fortnight later on 28th February there was yet another opening: Metrolink made it to Rochdale Railway Station (with stops at Newhey, Milnrow, Kingsway Business Park and Newbold), completing the re-opening of the former BR line. Around the same time, the Network Management Centre – Metrolink's control room – was relocated from the depot at Queens Road to the new one at Trafford.

Metrolink built into the central reservation on leaving Ashton Town Centre.

(Above): Julian Shaw and Jenny Crompton were so inspired by the tram stop sharing their names (Shaw and Crompton) they took a tram to their wedding reception!

By May the long-awaited Passenger Information Displays (PIDs) were switched on to show real-time departure information. Initially this was only on city centre stops, except for Mosley Street: it finally closed on Saturday 18th May. Dating from the original opening in 1992, it was the last single-direction stop and also still featured a profiled platform, which meant that only double T68 trams, with retractable steps, were equipped to use it and none of the new M5000s could. As there was no room to allow a full exten-

sion of the stop, it was removed entirely. A new double indicator PID was put in its place, to point people in the direction of the services available from the other Metrolink stops in the vicinity.

Far as it goes

The intensive period of growth continued again at the end of May 2013 as the rest of the South Manchester line opened to its current

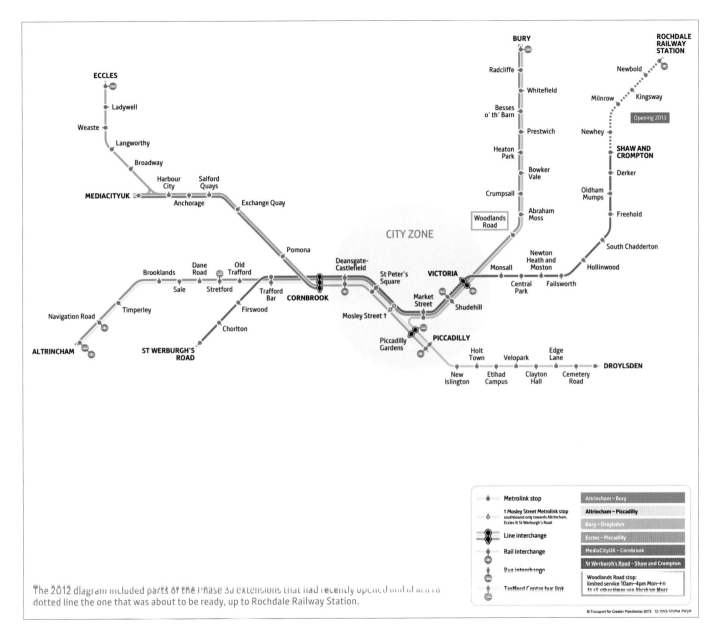

ECCLES

Ladywell

Weaste

Langworthy

Broadway

Harbour City
Salford Quays

MEDIACITYUK

Anchorage

Exchange Quay

Pomona

Brooklands
Dane Road
Old Trafford

Sale
Stretford

Trafford Bar

CORNBROOK

Firswood

Chorlton

Timperley

Navigation Road

ALTRINCHAM

ST WERBURGH'S ROAD

Deansgate-Castlefield

St Peter's Square

Mosley Street †

Piccadilly Gardens

PICCADILLY

Market Street

Shudehill

VICTORIA

Monsall

Central Park

Failsworth

CITY ZONE

Woodlands Road

BURY

Radcliffe

Whitefield

Besses o' th' Barn

Prestwich

Heaton Park

Bowker Vale

Crumpsall

Abraham Moss

Newton Heath and Moston

Hollinwood

South Chadderton

Freehold

Oldham Mumps

Derker

SHAW AND CROMPTON

Newhey

Milnrow
Kingsway

Newbold

ROCHDALE RAILWAY STATION

Opening 2013

Holt Town
Velopark
Edge Lane

New Islington
Etihad Campus
Clayton Hall
Cemetery Road

DROYLSDEN

	Metrolink stop
	† Mosley Street Metrolink stop southbound only towards Altrincham, Eccles & St Werburgh's Road
	Line interchange
	Rail interchange
	Bus interchange
	Trafford Centre bus link

Altrincham – Bury
Altrincham – Piccadilly
Bury – Droylsden
Eccles – Piccadilly
MediaCityUK – Cornbrook
St Werburgh's Road – Shaw and Crompton

Woodlands Road stop:
limited service 10am–4pm Mon–Fri
At all other times use Abraham Moss

© Transport for Greater Manchester 2012   12-1553-123754 75QJP

The 2012 diagram included parts of the Phase 3a extensions that had recently opened and shown in a dotted line the one that was about to be ready, up to Rochdale Railway Station.

OLDHAM MUMPS
Home of the Britain's shortest lived light rail stop

(Above): The strange case of Oldham Mumps. (Top left): Closed as a British Rail station in 2009. (Top right): conversion to light rail, 2011. (Bottom left): Open to Metrolink trams, June 2012. (Bottom right): Closed to trams January 2014 and here being demolished later that year. It was open for just 18 months.
(Opposite): What the temporary station was replaced with when the tracks were diverted to run though the heart of the town centre, the new Oldham Mumps.

terminus at East Didsbury. The extra 4.4km added four intermediate stops – Withington, Burton Road, West Didsbury and Didsbury
Village – to maximise access to services in this highly populated
area. Even from this far out, taking a tram is still quicker than a bus
and the line was likely to prove one of the network's busiest.

Powers to construct the so-called second city crossing (2CC) were
approved by the Government in October, and the same month
construction reached the point where it was permissible to allow
trams to be tested on the new tracks through the very centre of
Oldham. Similar trials had already been completed down the road
in Tameside, so on 9th October 2013, the Phase 3b extension from
Droylsden opened all the way to Ashton-under-Lyne via
Audenshaw, Ashton Moss and Ashton West, completing the East
Manchester line as well. In the final month of 2013 came yet more
network development news: at a meeting on December 6th, the
TfGMC outlined the long awaited full route for the 5.5km line into
Trafford Park, and ten days later the new stop which had been
constructed on the old staff-only halt at Queens Road was opened
to the public as a full stop on the Bury line: a boon for visitors to the
Greater Manchester Transport Museum and local residents and
businesses who had previously faced a long walk to any tram stop.

2014 has yet more growth

The New Year had barely begun when on 13th January 2014 prelim-
inary utility diversion work kicked off on the second city crossing.
By the end of that month, the new tracks laid through Oldham town
centre were ready to support regular passenger service. This short
section featured four new stops (Westwood, Oldham King Street,
Oldham Central and the new, permanent Oldham Mumps) and this
sealed the fate of the tunnels on the former branch line that had
housed the service since it first opened just a year and a half earlier.
Although the track itself was too old to be recycled elsewhere on
the system, some went to Heaton Park heritage tramway.

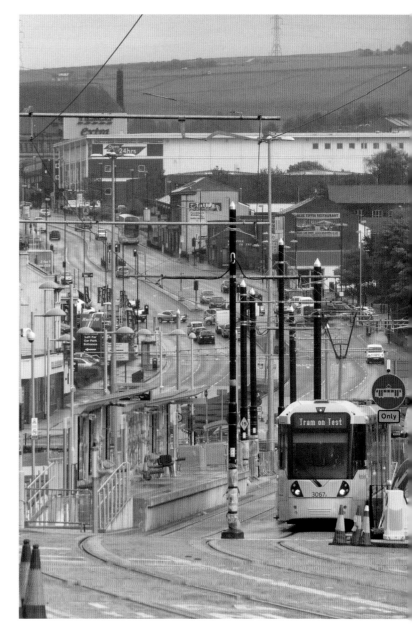

Greater Manchester tram network map

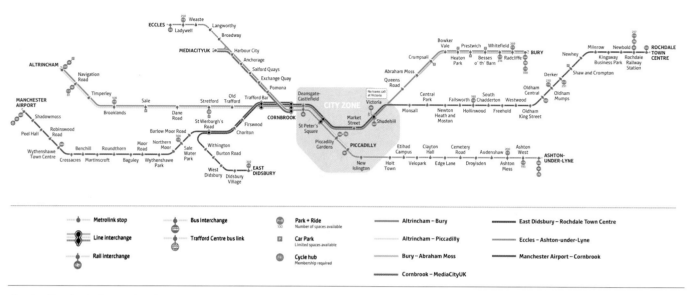

Legend

- Metrolink stop
- Line interchange
- Rail interchange
- Bus interchange
- Trafford Centre bus link
- Park + Ride — Number of spaces available
- Car Park — Limited spaces available
- Cycle hub — Membership required

- Altrincham – Bury
- Altrincham – Piccadilly
- Bury – Abraham Moss
- Cornbrook – MediaCityUK
- East Didsbury – Rochdale Town Centre
- Eccles – Ashton-under-Lyne
- Manchester Airport – Cornbrook

Greater Manchester tram network map

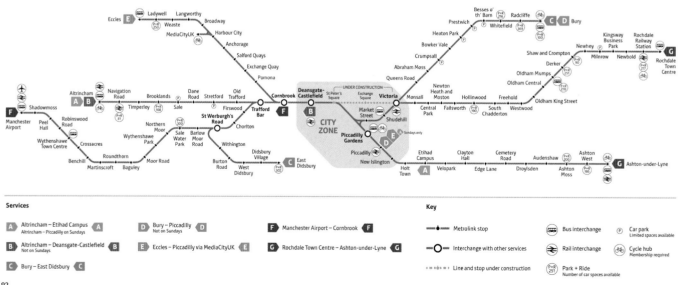

Services

- **A** Altrincham – Etihad Campus — Altrincham – Piccadilly on Sundays
- **B** Altrincham – Deansgate-Castlefield — Not on Sundays
- **C** Bury – East Didsbury
- **D** Bury – Piccadilly — Not on Sundays
- **E** Eccles – Piccadilly via MediaCityUK
- **F** Manchester Airport – Cornbrook
- **G** Rochdale Town Centre – Ashton-under-Lyne

Key

- Metrolink stop
- Interchange with other services
- Line and stop under construction
- Bus interchange
- Rail interchange
- Park + Ride — Number of car spaces available
- Car park — Limited spaces available
- Cycle hub — Membership required

(Opposite): before and after the map was altered to a single line colour, in 2014. (Above) the last T68 runs a special service for enthusiasts, May 2014.

Network Rail's plans to upgrade Victoria station included a dramatic new roof structure to replace the old, leaking one that had sat above the Metrolink platforms. The new roof construction was timed to coincide with the rebuilding of the Metrolink stop that was required to accommodate the forthcoming second city crossing and the resulting additional services that it would bring. The new stop would have two double faced platforms for the three tracks required, providing further benefits for the lines to Bury and Oldham/Rochdale. The work took 12 months to complete, during which time trams passed Victoria non-stop. An extensive information campaign was undertaken across the network to explain the need for passengers to change trams at Shudehill during this period.

Rochdale's new hydro-powered transport interchange had opened in November 2013 but as contractors were tidying up their Phase 3b work on this side of the conurbation, the final link in the puzzle – the long route from the railway station into Rochdale Town Centre – opened on 31st March 2014.

(Below): First tram leaving Cornbrook for the Airport, November 2014. (Above): Clean and simple, the River Mersey flood plain bridge at Sale Water Park.

(Above): Old and new side by side: Rochdale's town hall from the old bus station with new tram lines and interchange under construction, 2014.

Manchester Airport Stop

(Above): Progress at Manchester Airport. (Top row): before construction, 2013.
(Bottom left): During construction, late 2013 (Bottom right): open a year later.

The 68s T-off

After their 22 years of service and dominance of the city street-scape, the original T68 trams designed in the early 1990s were being phased out, slightly before the end of their expected lifespan.

Rolling stock engineer David Bielby told the author: "The problem was that they were built in Italy and didn't take account of the northern European climate: they did get very rusty 'under the bonnet''. [45] So on 26th May 2014 there was a farewell tour for the

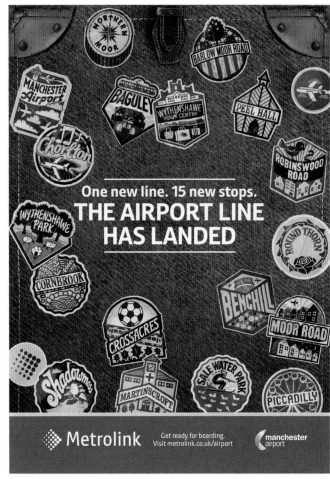

TfGM Airport line poster with stops as exotic-looking destination labels.

remaining T68s on their traditional routes: Piccadilly-Eccles, and Bury-Altrincham. There were even some limited edition tickets printed and sold to raise £3,400 for charity. Several hundred tram enthusiasts witnessed the start of the tour from the Piccadilly undercroft stop, where some of the original drivers from 1992 took charge of the two trams sporting their original uniforms. There was even a commemorative book on the T68s produced by Andrew Coward and John Henderson.

New maps for old

As the Metrolink grew from two lines into a network, the question arose of how best to display all the services on a map – a conundrum that faces the operators of all larger networks. The traditional solution of colouring each line differently was employed by TfGM from the launch in 1992 right up until 2014. But a new concept was introduced in 2015 by TfGM cartographer Simon Platt: "the idea was based on removing the potential complication of many coloured lines (they would all be in one grey hue) and showing 'services' with pointed flags". Simon told the author: "we don't have fixed lines like London Underground does, the services are quite flexible, especially as the system has been growing over the last few years". [46.] However in 2017, once service patterns had stabilised and due to popular demand, colours were reintroduced on the diagram".

Computer mock-up of the relocated St Peter's Square stop and 2CC.

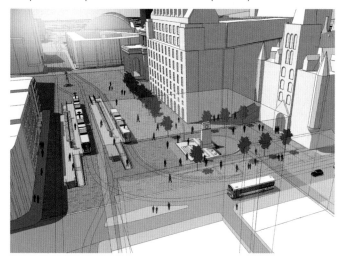

Euros for Exchange and shifting St Peter

The Chancellor is shown the underbelly of a tram at the new Trafford depot.

In June, the European Regional Development Fund agreed almost £11m to kick start the initial stage of the Second City Crossing (2CC) which would allow the first section from Victoria to Exchange Square to be built early, ahead of the full alignment which was due in 2017.

In a separate funding development, TfGM secured £50 million from the Local Growth Fund, the first tranche of money allocated to transport. The funding was able to buy a dozen new trams (a bigger number than first anticipated because of favourable currency exchange rates and purchasing in bulk). At this point it was now foreseen that the eventual number of M5000s would be more like 120: making it by far the largest light rail fleet in the UK.

Also in July, TfGM announced plans for relocating the pivotal St Peter's Square (SPS) stop. The changes were needed to allow more room and the ability for cross-platform interchange when 2CC went live. The original platforms, almost directly opposite the entrance to Central Library, would be demolished and moved closer to the proposed new junction onto Princess Street.

Here there would be two new island platforms providing trams at four platform faces. The Cenotaph, which had been at the original end of the square was also moved to the other end, placing it on the site of the former Peace Gardens (which were removed at an earlier date).

The construction works would require a complete shutdown of the St Peter's Square stop and a severing in half of the network on either side. The much smaller memorial cross, which marks the site of the ancient St Peter's church would remain in its current position and eventually sit neatly between the new tram tracks.

(Above): The full tram/bus interchange for Wythenshawe, opened July 2015.
(Below): A semi-rural feel as a test tram leaves Peel Hall, October 2014.

Take the tram to the plane and take over all transport

The end of 2014 saw no let-up in the expansion of the Metrolink network. On 3rd November trams began public service to Manchester Airport: a good 12 months ahead of schedule. Shadowmoss was the first stop out of the Airport, then: Peel Hall, Robinswood Road, Wythenshawe Town Centre, Crossacres, Benchill, Martinscroft, Roundthorn, Baguley, Moor Road, Wythenshawe Park, Northern Moor, Sale Water Park and Barlow Moor Road. Passengers on the ceremonial first early morning service were welcomed on board by cabin crew from EasyJet, Jet2, Monarch and Thomas Cook. But it was not the only surprise of the day: Chancellor George Osborne greeted staff at the new Trafford depot and sat in the driver's cab on the journey to the airport. Mr Osborne then made a major announcement: that Greater Manchester would be the beneficiary of the first major devolution of powers from central Government to the regions. Not only would the new powers bring more jurisdiction over the running of the bus services (similar to those enjoyed by the Mayor of London) but the Greater Manchester Combined Authority (GMCA) would get the

Exchange Square stop which was the first part of the 2CC to open.

(Both): A modern but environmentally friendly look at Deansgate-Castlefield refit includes a living wall and leaf motifs on the glass shelter canopies.

ability to fund and deliver the new Trafford Park line and properly integrated smartcard ticketing on all modes of transport – something long-dreamed for the conurbation.

Osborne's set-up also allowed for the possibility of planning for long-term local transport investment, providing access to up almost £1 billion over three decades. This could be allocated to initiatives to improve Metrolink, develop tram-train proposals and also improve the local rail network, an area where the GMCA's powers could also extend to in the foreseeable future.

With all this excitement in the air, the start of construction on 2CC almost got lost in November (except amongst tram enthusiasts and the teams inside TfGM) but it was certainly a fitting end to yet another monumental year for Metrolink.

(Above): Deansgate–Castlefield has room for three platforms following its refit. Note the grass-filled trackbed too. (Below) 'Safe To Sing' event, 2016 promoted equality after a homophobic attack on a tram.

2015/16: less expansion/more passengers

After such a long focus on growth, the next couple of years felt a bit calmer and it was not until the end of March 2015 that another big improvement was announced: free wifi was made available on all Metrolink services. On 13th June another milestone: the 100th new M5000 arrived at Queen's Road depot after its journey from Vienna.

At the end of June the St Peter's Square stop was completely closed for eight weeks to allow for its rebuild in preparation for 2CC. Again, a massive public information campaign was needed to keep customers informed of the changes to their journeys. A month later the new tram and bus interchange opened In Wythenshawe, and after yet another month, at the end of August, there had been enough ground work done to allow a single line to be opened through the St Peter's Square site: a great relief to Metrolink

(Below): Looking out on the new roof from an older arch in Victoria station. (Above): TramGB at Edge Lane. (Opposite): TfGM Transformation Information publicity.

customers as it meant that the network was joined up again. By mid-September work was completed on the rebuilding of Deansgate-Castlefield: a new feature lift had been added with an impressive green 'living' wall and platform capacity had been increased with further environmental features installed between the tracks. The final event of 2015 was an early Christmas present: the first stage of the 2CC was ready between Victoria and the new stop at Exchange Square. Situated in a prime location, between the historic Corn Exchange, the revitalised Printworks, the refurbished Arndale Centre and Selfridges store, this stop is set to become one of the network's busiest. Initially it was a terminus for services coming in from Victoria until 2CC was opened in full. The year 2016 undoubtedly saw disruption for passengers – but it was all for the

The Rainbow Tram attracted lots of social media activity, seen here in 2016.

good. The Eccles line (including the branch to MediaCity:UK) had to be closed for maintenance and services between St Peter's Square and Deansgate-Castlefield were temporarily suspended. However they were resumed just in time for the August Bank Holiday, when a tram had been covered in special colourful vinyl to celebrate the Manchester Pride events taking place in the city. The Rainbow Tram as it became known proved quite an attraction with many photos shared on social media. There was also a major safety campaign undertaken across the network after a horrific hate crime happened on a tram in 2015.

In mid October 2016 the Secretary of State for Transport gave TfGM the powers needed to build what many regard as the final link in the Metrolink system: the long hoped-for route to Trafford Park. The 5.5km line was set to cost £350 million and allow passengers direct access to the vast shopping mecca, now renamed the Intu Trafford Centre. Taking light rail to Dumplington, the name of the area where the Trafford Centre is located, had been an aspiration since the very earliest days of planning Metrolink. Later in the year M-Pact Thales (MPT) and WSP Parsons Brinckerhoff were chosen to deliver the extension. Ground was broken for the advance works early in 2017.

Olympic Gold and 2CC

Following the success of the British athletes at the 2016 Olympic Games, TfGM had a tram wrapped in gold coloured vinyl. The vehicle chosen was number 91 (from the fleet of 120) in recognition of the total number of gold medals won by both Team GB and ParalympicsGB. The golden tram was another source of selfies and many positive comments on social media especially on the day when the Heroes Parade passed through the city centre.

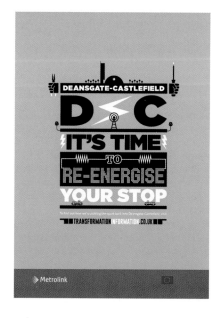

(Above): A view of Manchester's iconic Town Hall which some at the start of the light rail project could hardly have imagined: trams running again in Albert Square.

Meanwhile work on laying new track between St Peters Square and the Exchange Square stop was progressing so rapidly that by 1st December 2016, the last link in the second city crossing was ready to receive its first test tram.

By the end of February 2017 2CC was ready for its official public opening: the trams turned right out of the newly refurbished Victoria station, passed through the Exchange Square stop that had opened first, then continued along Cross Street through the centre of the area which had been so badly damaged twenty years before in the IRA bombing of the city, then left into Albert Square and right to join the other tracks in the newly enlarged St Peter's Square. Service patterns across the network were fine-tuned so that some ran over the new section and others ran down the Mosley Street section of track (sometimes known as '1CC').

25 years and counting

As the 25th anniversary of the opening of Metrolink approached, Peter Cushing, the Director who had overseen the huge expansion of the previous few years, took his chance to hand over the reins to his successor, Danny Vaughan, in March 2017. Vaughan, who had been Cushing's deputy since joining TfGM from LUAS (Dublin's light rail network) in 2013, began work straight away and one of his first tasks was announcing that a new operator would take over the running of Metrolink from RATP Dev in July 2017.

In preparation for the 25th Anniversary of the system opening (6th April 2017) a tram was applied with a special livery featuring the number '25' in the Metrolink speed pattern. During an event announcing an anniversary project in the Bridgewater Hall on that day, the special tram passed by tooting merrily. The event heralded the start of 'Tram Tracks' – a huge project for local artists and musicians to write a piece of music or spoken word for every single one of the 93 Metrolink stops: a big task. Many of them were perfomed at two gala concerts during July 2017 at the Bridgewater Hall.

(Above): Livery to commemorate the 25th anniversary was applied to tram 3092.
(Right): Chocolate bar given to passengers on the day.

Metrolink has come a long way since those early days and is now carrying almost 40 million passengers annually over seven lines and on 92 km of track. Almost 400 drivers are employed for its 120 vehicles, allowing up to 90 trams per hour through the busiest stops. Moreover it has undoubtedly proved the case for the viability of light rail in Britain and, as the next chapter will show, it has great plans ahead for the next 25 years.

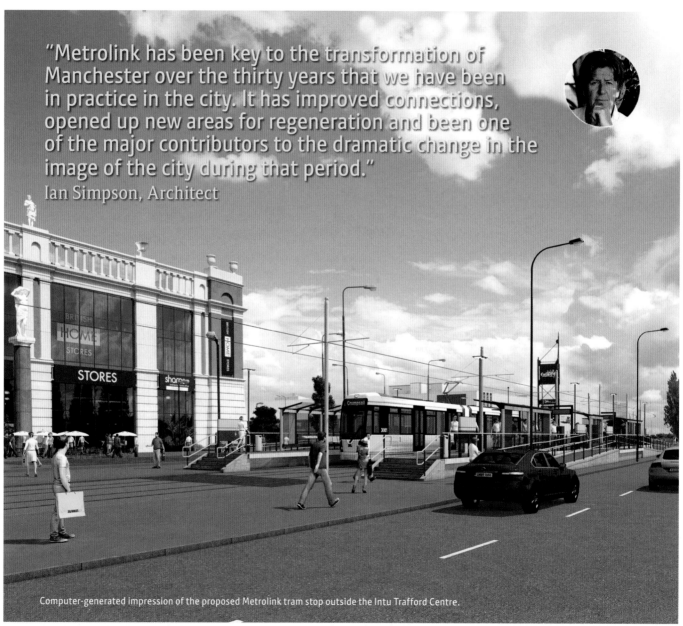

"Metrolink has been key to the transformation of Manchester over the thirty years that we have been in practice in the city. It has improved connections, opened up new areas for regeneration and been one of the major contributors to the dramatic change in the image of the city during that period."
Ian Simpson, Architect

Computer-generated impression of the proposed Metrolink tram stop outside the Intu Trafford Centre.

Completing the Network

As the 25th anniversary kicked off in 2017, and the second city crossing was opened, work also began on what some say may be the last major extension of the Metrolink tram network in its current form: the long awaited route to Trafford Park.

Situated on the south side of the Manchester Ship Canal, it was the world's first planned industrial estate – and still remains the largest of its kind in Europe. As such it has an impressive history: it was home to heavy engineering company Westinghouse, later renamed as Metropolitan-Vickers, who set up a radio station at their factory in 1922 (which became Britain's first regular BBC regional radio broadcaster, 2ZY, opened a day after London's 2LO); Ford had their first assembly plant for Model T cars in Trafford Park: and during the war it became the manufacturing base for ICI's penicillin and for the production of Avro Manchester and Avro Lancaster bombers. Rolls-Royce Merlin engines were built there and Kelloggs has its largest factory on the estate and was headquartered there.

At its peak in 1945, some 75,000 people worked in Trafford Park but it suffered from the same long term decline as many other British manufacturing hubs. By the late 1980s the concept of out-of-town shopping centres was gathering momentum in the UK. Not dissimilar from the malls that had festooned American suburbs, they were widely perceived as a threat to traditional High Streets, and opposed by many local authorities – including Manchester City Council. One of the first to open was the enormous MetroCentre in Gateshead, but contrary to its name, the centre is not directly connected to the Tyne & Wear Metro. So when the idea arose for property developers to transform a vast site to the west of Trafford Park itself, and with knowledge that a light rail scheme was coming to the region, initial plans for the shopping centre included suggested routes for what became Metrolink.

The planning and construction of the centre took much longer than originally anticipated – it did not open until 1998 – by which time

Part of bustling Trafford Park beside the ship canal, 1930s

funding for the Metrolink line had dried up. Commercial concerns decided against contributing to light rail construction, although by then, the Metrolink concept was so well established with local authorities that the projected route had been 'safeguarded' and at Pomona, when the Eccles branch was under construction in 1999, accommodation had been built-in for a turn out for future tracks in the direction of Trafford Park. This foresight turned out to be another Central Park-type move. Although the Trafford Park line did not feature in the funded sections of the Big Bang expansion, aspirations to get Metrolink to the shopping centre (and beyond) have remained a long term objective.

Several paths

The initial trajectory for the line took it into the heart of one of the oldest parts of the Trafford Park estate, The Village, and along Westinghouse Road and beside the Bridgewater Canal. For several years there was an aspiration to take the line through Giants Field and Lostock Parkway was also a proposed station site for some time. But subsequent reconfiguring by TfGM forged several different trajectories and stop locations and it was these that went to public consultation during 2014. The revised route was less convoluted and also shorter and therefore less expensive.

TRAFFORD PARK IS WAITING FOR THE MET

The route of the Trafford Park line, under construction as this book went to press: (Top left): where the tracks will leap off the bridge at Pomona and drop down to the canalside. (Top right): route of the old Docks railway which will be taken over by Metrolink. (Bottom left): the pub is to be demolished but the island (a former podium for a swing bridge) may stay. (Bottom right): another section of the old railway line where trams will one day run.

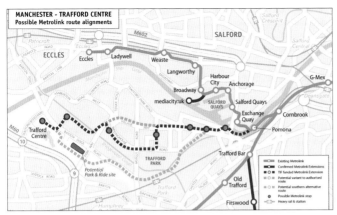

Showing alternative routes considered such as Westinghouse Road.

Built in 1999 with the Eccles line: the future junction to Trafford Park.

In fact there have been at least three variants of the Trafford Park route over the years. Two important businesses raised some concerns about it: ITV Studios and Manchester United. One had fears over potential noise issues during the filming of Coronation Street, and the other about peak traffic flows on match days. With anxieties calmed, in 2016 a Transport & Works Order was finally received for the 5.5km line with six new stops, so initial clearance work and utility diversion could begin on 12th January 2017.

In common with parts of the route to Wythenshawe, some sections had been designated for tramways for so long that the line will feel almost segregated from other users (along the Ship Canal between Pomona and Imperial War Museum, and beside Parkway for example), but elsewhere (along Village Way and Trafford Wharf Road) the trams will feel more like they are running on the street among traffic, as the Eccles and Ashton lines do. Part of the route nearest to where it peels off from the Eccles line at Pomona will also

In the 2016 proposals, several stops had moved location and Giants Field was dropped in favour of Event City. The line also shifted from Mosley Road.

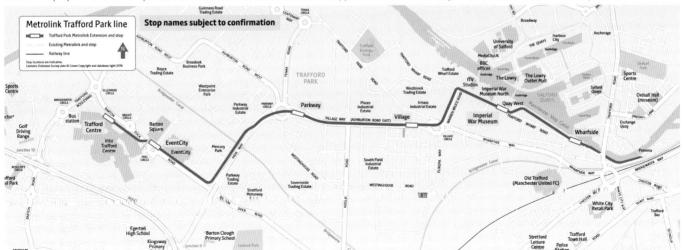

If the Trafford Park line is extended to Port Salford it will cross the Ship Canal via this lifting bridge on which space will be left for the tram tracks, when finished.

A proposed stop at Lostock Parkway will no longer be on the route.

be on the alignment of the former Manchester Ship Canal railway freight lines. The stop names will be Wharfside, Imperial War Museum, Village, Parkway, Event City, Trafford Centre.

Beyond the waters

Several viable trajectories to push the line on from what is proposed to be the terminal outside the Intu Trafford Centre have also been evaluated. One which made it on to early maps was Port Salford. This is a huge new freight terminal which opened in 2016 and was built by the Peel Group to maximise the potential of the Manchester Ship Canal in relation to the UK Motorway network. It is destined to be an area which could become home to many thousands of jobs. Cited as being part of the even larger Atlantic Gateway project (to boost both Liverpool and Manchester), new road and rail links were also proposed under the Western Gateway Infrastructure Scheme. The Metrolink extension would run west-

Artist's impression of the proposed Metrolink stop at Imperial War Museum on the new Trafford Park line.

wards from the Trafford centre to a new stop provisionally called Trafford Quays to serve a leisure development (not yet built but planning permission has been granted). A convoluted route would then take the tracks across the M60 Motorway to the next projected stop beside the Salford Reds rugby stadium – provisionally entitled Salford City Stadium. Another complex route would then take the line over the Manchester Ship Canal on a new lifting bridge currently under construction into Port Salford itself where it would terminate. This section remains unfunded at time of writing (2017).

There is still an active policy intention from Salford City Council (in the authority's unitary development plan) to extend the Eccles line from beyond its current terminus, along the A57 to Barton-upon-Irwell and then across the Manchester Ship Canal to meet the Trafford Park Line terminus outside the shopping centre. Funding is being examined from various sources.

Taking it further

Over the years many other extensions have been proposed to the Metrolink network. Although they **do not represent TfGM policy**, here is a summary of the most discussed:

• Stockport

This is the longest standing aspiration dating back to the pre-Metrolink construction days. In the mid-1990s the plan was to head into the town via the Pyramid building. More recent local authority safeguards are placed further south but crossing the Motorway is the most expensive part. This may be superseded by Tram-Train.

• Wythenshawe loop

Completion of the proposed western side of the original loop which enters the previously constructed tunnel at the end of the line of the current terminal at Manchester Airport. It could now include a stop at the new Terminal building, the Airport City Enterprise Zone

All the recently refurbished city centre stops have been delivered to high capacity standards ready for increased passenger traffic from future extensions.

Would a Greater Manchester tram-train look something like this? Steve Nicklin's mock up of a Vossloh Class 399 Light Rail Vehicle.

and then one alongside the HS2 Airport station (possibly to be named as Manchester Interchange). It would then continue on what was its original trajectory towards Davenport Green, Wythenshawe Hospital, and Newall Green rejoining the existing line just south of the Roundthorn stop. Some claim it is more likely to happen due to the benefits it could bring by linking with the HS2 line station.

• **Middleton**
Rochdale Metropolitan Borough Council proposal to build a branch off the Bury line from Bowker Vale stop to Middleton town centre. In a separate proposal to reach Middleton, Oldham West and Royton MP Jim Mahon proposed in 2016 that a spur could be built from Westwood tram stop on the existing OLR route and pass through the centre onto the other proposed line (from the Bury line) to rejoin at Bowker Vale – forming a new loop.

• **Ashton to Oldham**
Mahon also proposed a link between Ashton-under-Lyne tram stop and Oldham using part of another abandoned track bed (part of the former Oldham, Ashton and Guide Bridge railway – closed to passengers in 1959).

• **Stalybridge**
A short extension from the current terminus of the Ashton line into the centre of Stalybridge was proposed by Tameside Metropolitan Borough Council in 2011, but support for the idea has dissipated.

• **Tyldesley loopline**
Reopening a line closed to passengers in 1969 under the Beeching cuts. It ran from Eccles through Patricroft, Worsley, Tyldesley, and Leigh (and on to Newton-le-Willows). The idea would have been to extend tracks from the existing Eccles Metrolink terminus to join the old trackbed and follow it round to Little Hulton via Walkden.

• **Inner south Manchester/University**
Acknowledged as one of the most obvious corridors for light rail since 1960s proposals, the route from the city centre to the University campus (sometimes referred to as the Oxford Road corridor), and beyond to Rusholme, Fallowfield and possibly Didsbury, is still a hot topic for enthusiasts but not an active strategy for TfGM at the present time (although it may be studied in the future).

• **In-fill stops**
A number of stops on existing lines (or one where they were first discussed but later dropped/resited) still garner interest on online forums. Buckley Wells (between Bury and Radcliffe) appeared on several aspirational maps in the 1990s/2000s. There was always supposed to be a stop between Rochdale Railway Station and the Town Centre Interchange at Drake Street. Several stops on the Airport Line didn't make it to final plans (Hough End, Hardy Farm, Haveley and Woodhouse Park). Campaigners still hope for a stop on the 2CC between St Peters Square and Exchange Square (on Cross Street, possibly close to King Street). The most likely major focus will however be on a new breed of light rail vehicle: the Tram-Train.

Is it a tram or a train?

Looking forward, one of the interesting areas of potential development for Metrolink is a new breed of light rail vehicle: the tram-train. Following changes to the British Rail network in south/east Manchester (especially the introduction of the Hazel Grove Chord), two of the routes originally proposed for conversion to Metrolink were deemed as no longer viable: Glossop/Hadfield and Marple/Rose Hill. When the concept of introducing European style tram-trains into the UK began to be discussed in the Noughties, GMPTE was an early adopter of the idea. By using the city centre tram tracks it looked like it might be possible to link rail services from the north/west (the line to Wigan via Atherton) onto those routes to Glossop and Marple, allowing some traditional BR heavy rail

Tram-Train trials in Sheffield, 2017. Could vehicles like this be running across Greater Manchester in the future?

services to share the outlying tracks and the new tram-trains to run through the city centre to connect up the services. In this way several new long and profitable routes could be added to Metrolink with no need to build much more than a few spurs from main lines onto tram tracks. The idea had been successfully tried in Karlsruhe, a city which gave much inspiration to the construction of Metrolink in its formative years. Others like Cagliari, Grenoble, Kassal, Lyon, Mulhouse, Paris, and Porto have all introduced tram-trains in recent years. The Department for Transport proposed a diesel vehicle trial for the UK, but as they wanted to test low-floor vehicles, the Penistone Line (Sheffield to Huddersfield) was chosen in 2008. It would have had no physical connection to existing Supertram tracks in Sheffield (and also fell foul of European pollution rules) so was quickly ruled out. A £51 million pilot tram-train

scheme that does spur off the Sheffield system is now under way to link the city with neighbouring Rotherham.

A feasibility study undertaken by TfGM in 2013 examined a number of potential tram-train routes:
· Manchester – Bredbury – Marple
· Manchester – Glossop
· Manchester – Atherton – Wigan
· Manchester – Sale – Altrincham – Hale/Knutsford
· Manchester – East Didsbury – Hazel Grove
· Stockport – Altrincham
The Marple one received the most favourable analysis and has been proposed for the initial phase of tram-train development in Greater Manchester. The routes to Glossop and Hazel Grove would probably

Manchester Airport T2 building: this is the potential site of a future Metrolink stop if the western section of the Wythenshawe loop is constructed.

form Phase 2. Although the Stockport–Altrincham alignment did not demonstrate such great benefits as a stand-alone scheme, it was thought worthy of returning to when HS2 and Airport investment occurs. Wigan was singled out as the one with the greatest scope for more study over possible alignments. The idea to extend to Hale/ Knutsford was not proposed for further development at this time.

Going round in circles and filling holes

Since that report, and taking on board various suggestions from the public and politicians, there has been increased discussion about linking the outlying towns and suburbs together without the need to go into the regional centre: creating a form of circle line. TfGM have undertaken some feasibility studies and concluded that at least some sections of what is being dubbed the Orbital route would indeed be technically possible and desirable. Combining tram-train, standard Metrolink and potentially some other systems, there is now active investigation of routes between Altrincham to Bolton via Stockport, Ashton, Oldham, Rochdale and Bury.

The other area that was not addressed in the 2013 report was how (or even if) the vehicles would cross the city and connect to each other (which was, after all, one of the main purposes for considering tram-train technology in the first place). Since the opening of 2CC, the creation of Transport for the North and the idea of a HS3 (to link Liverpool via Manchester with Leeds and other northern cities), and subsequent papers planning the future for the region (especially the Greater Manchester Spatial Framework and its vision for 2040): long-term thinking seems to have shifted away from the idea of building any more standard tram lines (in central Manchester at least), mainly due to road space. So in a wonderful twist of fate, the talk now is that Metrolink has proved itself so convincingly that for any new, third crossing of the centre: it would probably have to be made in tunnel. The dreamers of the previous century would rejoice could they but see it, but Manchester's future urban rail could very well be under the ground, after all.

Ed Howes fantasy future Metrolink network circa 2040

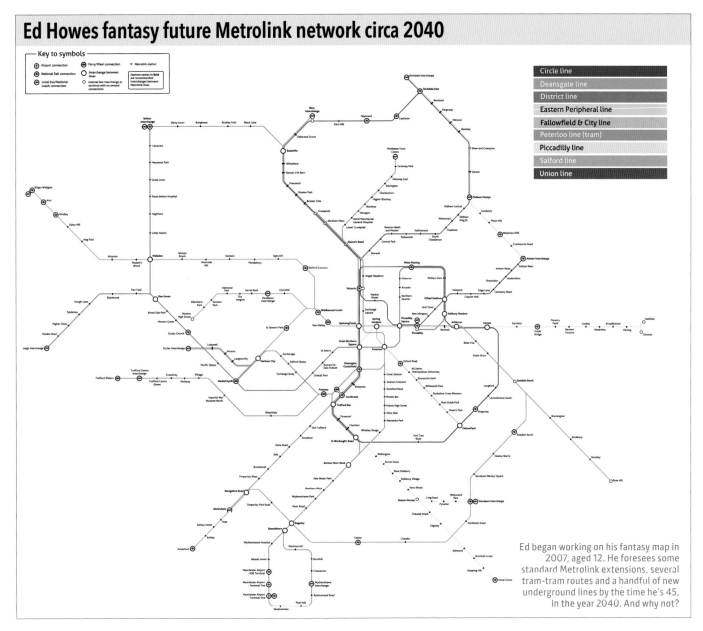

Ed began working on his fantasy map in 2007, aged 12. He foresees some standard Metrolink extensions, several tram-tram routes and a handful of new underground lines by the time he's 45, in the year 2040. And why not?

"I now live and work facing these tracks and love watching the trams every day helping to drive Manchester's ongoing regeneration"
Tom Bloxham, Property Developer

Catalyst for growth

Trams to transform a city

Before each funding round, authorities responsible for the city region's transport strategy were required to explain how Metrolink would bring jobs, prosperity and environmental improvements. In technical terms: a good cost/benefit ratio. Such projections are tricky to get right, but here economists and developers explain how and why the growth of a reliable public transport network has brought such step changes that the Greater Manchester region has experienced bigger improvements than any other urban area outside the prospering South.

From a fairly low point in the 1970s, the North West is now second only to London and the South East in terms of the Gross Value Added (GVA) generated for the UK economy – growing by 3.6% in 2015 (compared to the UK average of 2.9%). Not all of this is attributable to Manchester, or Metrolink of course, but given there were zero journeys made on urban rail in the conurbation in 1991, and now there are over 30 million annually, it stands to reason that the Metrolink network makes a significant contribution. But what has it achieved in economic terms? A 2014 survey by the Nationwide Building Society showed that house prices within a 500m radius of a Metrolink stop attracted a 4.6% increase in value for the advantages of good transport access. Robert Gardner, Nationwide's Chief Economist, said: "In Greater Manchester, 69% of properties are within 1,500m of a station and our research illustrates that people are willing to pay a modest premium to be close [to one]." [48.] A report by Lambert Smith Hampton said: "Manchester city centre is the most active UK office market outside Central London". [49.]

One of the most noticeable landmarks of the last decade was the arrival of the huge 169m Beetham Tower – at the time of opening in 2006, it boasted the highest residential address in the country. Architect Ian Simpson has said that its location beside the Deansgate-Castlefield Metrolink stop was a factor in choosing the site. The building became a symbol of the city's regeneration which

Actor William Roache at a tram naming ceremony, 2010.

over the last 15-20 years has been quite remarkable. Over and over again, the presence of Metrolink and particularly its expansion into a full network, is cited by property developers as a reason to invest in the city.

In fact Greater Manchester, is undergoing unprecedented change. The biggest ones can be seen on both sides of the River Irwell – where the cities of Manchester and Salford meet – and around the Quays where both the Trafford and Salford sides of the Manchester Ship Canal have seen massive amounts of development. The city

Deansgate-Castlefield stop overlooked by Ian Simpson's
Beetham Tower: a major symbol of city centre regeneration

region has been leading the way for the construction of new office space with more and taller skyscrapers than any other conurbation outside London. There are currently eight towers over 100m built or under construction (one at 200m) and another 20 of these in the pipeline (one at 237m – a tad higher than London's Canary Wharf). In the brochures of all these towers, copious mention is made of each development's proximity to a Metrolink stop: the value of the network being seen as a key selling point as much as the proximity of a Tube station might be in London. In 2015, for example, commercial property investment topped £1.5bn in Manchester. [51.] It caused Holly Brown of Commercial Property Blog to claim: "Massive infrastructure improvements to the Metrolink have played a significant part in attracting investment into Manchester, as well as attracting international investors seeking deals outside of London". [52.] More recently, in March 2017, Savills called it "a hot-spot for overseas buyers". [53.]

Filling the centre

Before the arrival of Metrolink, fewer than 300 people lived in the city centre (1987 figure). In 2017 this figure had rocketed to over 25,000, with the number set to double again in the next few years. If all currently planned projects reach fruition, almost 230,000 new homes and 2.4 million sqm of office space will be added to the conurbation by 2025. This on top of the thousands of apartments and square metres of office space created in the last 25 years since Metrolink opened. The Greater Manchester population is expected to top 3 million in the next decade. With outstanding growth figures that are bettered only by Greater London, no other major conurbation is even coming close to Greater Manchester for this level of development at the moment. Around 150,000 people now work in the city centre – a major increase from pre-Metrolink days – and around one third of those commute in to the city via tram.

Greg Rusedski, showing just how popular the trams have become with high profile figures. A number of other celebrities have contributed their voices to be used on public announcements. Kenneth Branagh was the voice used during Manchester International Festival in 2013. Four Manchester City footballers had theirs used for the launch of the East Manchester line in 2013: at Piccadilly Vincent Kompany was the voice, New Islington had Joe Hart, Holt Town had James Milner and Etihad Campus had Roberto Mancini. Brian Cox recorded several during 2016's 'Science In The City' week and Shaun Ryder's was used on BBC Music Day, 2017.

Metrolink trams have become icons for the city on souvenirs.

Cultural icons

Beyond purely economic benefits it is more difficult to get concrete figures. The city is home to a vast array of sporting and cultural venues, theatres and concert halls, hotel and conference facilities, the biggest retail centre outside London and numerous clubs/bars/restaurants. Metrolink provides access to this wealth of attractions for the local population as well as to the over 1 million overnight visitors who come to the city every year (a figure only bettered in the UK by London and Edinburgh). Although travelling to Manchester is undeniably more business, entertainment and sports related than, say, Edinburgh or Bath, with their more obvious pull to American sightseers, there are plenty of examples of souvenirs produced for visitors, and increasingly the Metrolink trams have become cultural icons representing the city.

Even outside the core areas, big improvements are also visible. The town centres of Oldham and Rochdale are good examples of where regeneration is taking hold, with long-planned new developments becoming a reality. Given that some of Britain's poorest wards lie in Greater Manchester, it is a testament to the planners that their foresight and determination in bringing light rail to Manchetser is helping to bring real prosperity to the city region.

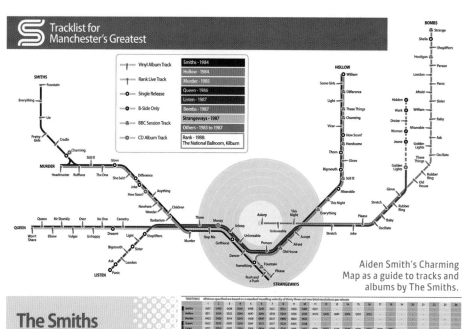

Aiden Smith's Charming Map as a guide to tracks and albums by The Smiths.

A crucial link for visitors and locals alike: St Peter's Square with its four platform faces is one of the key stops on the network.

When the map of a system starts being plagiarised, imitated or used out of context, it is yet another sign that the system is embedded into the fabric of city life. That happened with London's celebrated Tube map years ago, and increasingly it has been the case with the maps of other networks from Paris to Chicago. Interestingly this is now the case for the Metrolink too. Anagram maps of Manchester appeared in the 2000s (where cheeky or playful stop names are substituted for the real ones), but now full facsimiles of the diagram are being adapted for pub-stops, house price changes or in the case of one classic Manchester pop group: a track list for their entire back-catalogue.

With the trams now whizzing past so much of the conurbation; with such a regularity and reliability of service; with another line under construction; with the possibility of tram-trains to bring other routes and neighbourhoods within easy reach of fast and frequent urban rail services, it is finally true that Greater Manchester is getting the levels of public transport that it deserves.

Metrolink has been instrumental in making all this possible and will continue to contribute to building a better life for millions of people, locals and visitors alike, in the next 25 years of its story.

Index, Bibliography, Credits

Image Credits

Front cover: TfGM

Alex Hill: 2, 4. Andrew L. Roberts: 71. Author Collection: 9, 16, 25, 26, 28, 34, 42, 43, 49, 53, 71, 72, 87, 90, 100, 105, 106, 113, 120-124. Bombardier Transportation UK/Bombardier Transportation Austria GmbH: 55. Brook/Dodge Collection: 13, 15, 17. Capital Transport Collection: 6, 11. Chris Allen: 67. Dalton Maag: 58. David Tibke: 18. Design Triangle: 57. Ed Howes: 117. Greater Manchester Fire Service: 42. Greater Manchester Museum of Transport Collection: 12, 14, 27. Haywood Collection: 19, 26, 29-31. Hemisphere Agency: 57-61, 63, 70, 82. Howard Wilde: 18, 24, 32. ITV Studios: 80. Jan Chlebik: 70. John E. Henderson: 67, 93. Jonty Wilde: 57. Laura Kidd, 5. Macarthy Collection: 6, 33, 39, 44, 51, 62, 63, 65, 66, 71, 72, 74-79, 82-87,90.91, 93-98, 102, 104, 110-112, 118, 123, 124. Manchester City Council Archives: 5, 7-11, 15,16, 39, 109. Manchester City Football Club: 121. Manchester Evening News: 34, 42, 44. Paul Wolfgang Webster: 120 ProofSpirit (Aiden Smith): 122. Robert Pritchard: 115. Robson Collection: 36, Senior Collection: 29, 31, 32. Simpson Haugh: 108. Space Digital: 80. Steer Davies Gleave: 56. Steve Nicklin/Vossloh SG: 114. Steven Willets: 67. Transport for Greater Manchester/GMPTE Collection: 1, 3, 14, 21, 24, 30, 32, 34, 36-38, 40, 41, 43-48, 50, 52, 54-56, 62-64, 66, 69, 70, 73, 88, 89, 92, 93, 97, 97, 99, 101, 103, 105, 107, 108, 111-114, 119, 121, 123, 128. TriMet: 23. Urban Splash: 118. Vince Lowe: 101. Wikimedia Foundation/Creative commons licence: 3 (Essex Uni), 22, 29 (RL GNZLZ), 35 (Mikey-Flickr), 48 (Financial Times), 66, 67. Young Collection: 20, 21, 24, 27, 28

References

1. City Council minutes, 1868. And MEN 12/5/1977
2. City Council minutes, 27/11/1878. And MEN 12/5/1977
3. Manchester Courier, 05/05/1903
4. City Council minutes, 1912
5. Manchester Guardian, 1 Feb 1924
6-13. MEN 12/5/1977
14. Brook, Richard and Dodge, Martin, Infa-Manc Catalogue, p.132
15. Tony Beard, By Tube Beyond Edgware, 2001
16-22 Interviews with author, March/April 2017
23. David Holt, Manchester Metrolink, p.13
24-26. Interviews with author, March/April 2017
27. David Holt, Manchester Metrolink, p.27
28-31. Interviews with author, March/April 2017
32. Proposed Light Rail Schemes in Leeds, Manchester and South Hampshire, 2007, p. 5
33. Hansard, 10/12/2002, p. 155
34-39. Interviews with author, March/April 2017
40. Greater Manchester Future Transport report
41. The Coalition: our programme for government, HMSO, 2010, p.31
42-46. Interviews with author, March/April 2017
47. Nationwide House Price Index Special report 2014,
48. The Northern Powerhouse Office Market Report 2015/16
49. Lambert Smith Hampton, 2015
50. Interview with author, May 2017
51-52. www.novaloca.com 09/03/2016
53. www.savills.co.uk 22/03/2017

Bibliography

21 Years of Metrolink, supplement to Tramways & Urban Transit, 2013
A History of Manchester's Tramways, Souvenir Brochure, Manchester Corporation Transport Department, 1949
Beard, Tony, By Tube Beyond Edgware, Capital Transport, Harrow, 2001
Best, W.H. and Gillham, J.C., The Tramways of South-East Lancashire, Light Railway Transport League, 1976
Brook, Richard and Dodge, Martin, Infa-Manc Catalogue, Bauprint,Prestwich, 2012
Coward, Andrew and Henderson, John E, Superb – A Tribute to the Manchester Metrolink T68 and T68A Light Rail Vehicles, self-published, 2014
Gray, Ted and Kirby, Arthur, Manchester Trams, Castlefield Publications, Manchester
Holt, David, Manchester Metrolink, Platform Five, Sheffield, 1992
Joyce, J, Roads & rails of Manchester 1900-1950, Ian Allan, Shepperton, 1982
Kidd, Alan and Wyke, Terry, Manchester: Making The Modern City, LUP, Liverpool, 2016
National Audit Office, Proposed Light Rail Schemes in Leeds, Manchester and South Hampshire, Department of Transport, London, 2007.
Public Transport Plan for the Future, SELNEC PTE, Manchester, 1973
Railway Study Group, Report, Manchester, 1983
——, Interim Report of the Preferred Strategy, Manchester 1984
——, The Case for Light Rail, Manchester, 1984
Senior, John and Ogden, Eric, Metrolink, Transport Publishing Company, Glossop 1992
——, Metrolink Official handbook, Transport Publishing Company, Glossop 1991
Warrender, Keith, Underground Manchester, Willow Publishing, Timperley, 2007
——, Below Manchester, Willow Publishing, Timperley, 2009
Yearsley, Ian, The Manchester Tram, Advertiser Press, Huddersfield, 1962

Webography

• Greater Manchester Museum of Transport:
http://www.gmts.co.uk
• Manchester Archives:
http://images.manchester.gov.uk/index.php?session=pass
• Manchester Confidential:
http://confidentials.com/manchester/
• Manchester Evening News:
http://www.manchestereveningnews.co.uk/news/
• Metrolink homepage:
http://www.metrolink.co.uk
• Skyscrapercity.com Metrolink general forum:
http://www.skyscrapercity.com/showthread.php?t=584932
• Skyscrapercity.com Metrolink extension forum:
http://www.skyscrapercity.com/showthread.php?t=866944
• TfGM homepage:
http://www.tfgm.com

22/05/2017

22 people died when Manchester was attacked.
This book was being assembled over that period.
It is dedicated to the people whose lives were affected by the atrocity and the
Emergency Services, TfGM, Metrolink, Railway staff and ordinary people who assisted them.
"This...is the place"
Poet Longfella, Albert Square Vigil, 23/05/2017.